MW00899523

The Latest Instant Pot

Cookbook for Beginners

1600+ Quick & Healthy Instapot Recipes with One-Pot Wonders and Time-Saving Delights

Carlee W. Voight

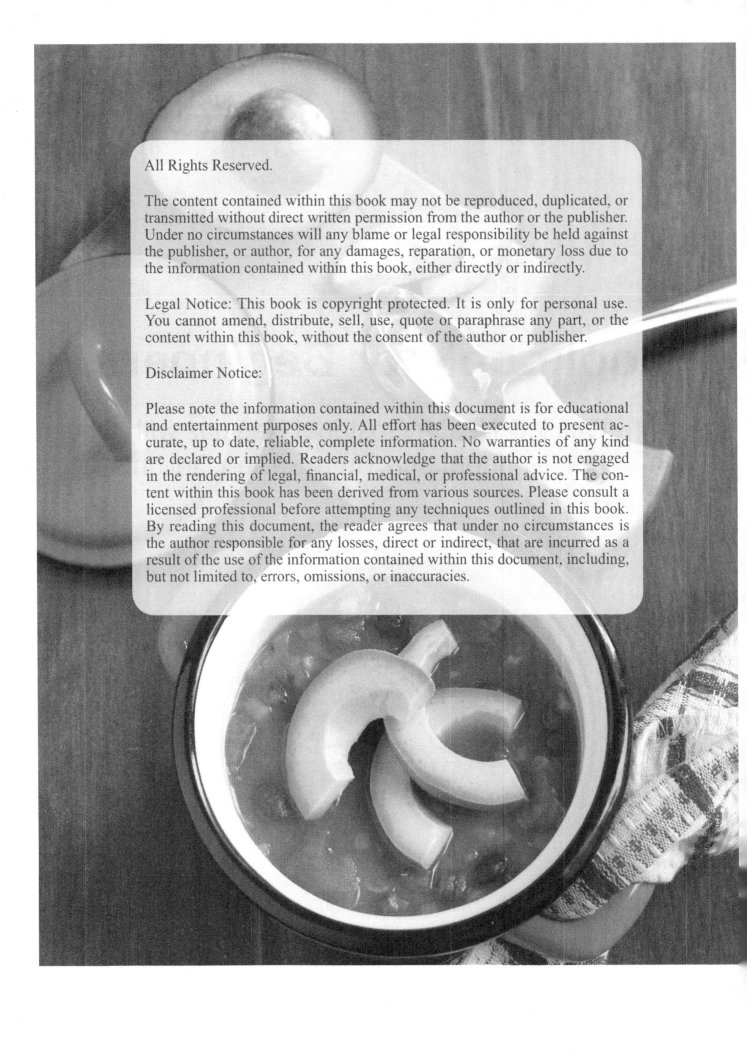

All Rights Reserved.

The content contained within this book may not be reproduced, duplicated, or transmitted without direct written permission from the author or the publisher. Under no circumstances will any blame or legal responsibility be held against the publisher, or author, for any damages, reparation, or monetary loss due to the information contained within this book, either directly or indirectly.

Legal Notice: This book is copyright protected. It is only for personal use. You cannot amend, distribute, sell, use, quote or paraphrase any part, or the content within this book, without the consent of the author or publisher.

Disclaimer Notice:

Please note the information contained within this document is for educational and entertainment purposes only. All effort has been executed to present accurate, up to date, reliable, complete information. No warranties of any kind are declared or implied. Readers acknowledge that the author is not engaged in the rendering of legal, financial, medical, or professional advice. The content within this book has been derived from various sources. Please consult a licensed professional before attempting any techniques outlined in this book. By reading this document, the reader agrees that under no circumstances is the author responsible for any losses, direct or indirect, that are incurred as a result of the use of the information contained within this document, including, but not limited to, errors, omissions, or inaccuracies.

CONTENTS

Chapter 5 Pork, Beef & Lamb 42

Chapter 8 Beans, Rice, & Grains...72

Chapter 9 Desserts & Drinks 82

INTRODUCTION

Welcome to the world of easy and delicious cooking with the Instant Pot! This Instant Pot cookbook is a collection of 1600 flavorful and nutritious recipes that will change your life in the kitchen. Whether you're a busy professional, a busy parent, or just someone who loves to cook, this cookbook is the perfect guide to make your life easier and more delicious.

With 1600 days worth of recipes, you'll never run out of meal ideas. From breakfast to dinner, appetizers to desserts, this cookbook has it all. You'll discover new and creative ways to use your Instant Pot, making it your go-to kitchen appliance for everything from quick weeknight meals to impressive dinner party dishes.

The recipes are organized by meal type and include helpful tips and tricks for cooking with your Instant Pot. You'll find recipes for classic dishes, as well as new and exciting recipes that will keep you coming back for more.

Inside this cookbook, you'll find recipes that are both easy and satisfying, without sacrificing flavor or nutrition:

1600 easy-to-follow recipes, including breakfasts, main courses, sides, desserts, and more.

A comprehensive guide to using your Instant Pot, including tips and tricks for getting the best results.

Nutritional information for every recipe, so you can keep track of your daily intake.

Recipes that are designed to be healthy, budget-friendly, and family-friendly.

Whether you're a beginner or an experienced Instant Pot user, this cookbook has everything you need to create delicious meals for any occasion. So, fire up your Instant Pot and get ready to impress your family and friends with your amazing cooking skills!

Chapter 1 Basic Information of 1600 Recipes Instant Pot Cookbook

What's the difference between a pressure cooker and an Instant Pot?

A pressure cooker is a standalone appliance that uses pressure cooking technology to cook food quickly and efficiently. It typically has a single function and is operated manually.

On the other hand, an Instant Pot is a brand of multi-functional electric pressure cooker that combines the functions of a pressure cooker, slow cooker, rice cooker, steamer, sauté pan, yogurt maker, and more. It is operated by an electric control panel that allows for precise temperature and pressure control, and it has pre-set programs for different types of cooking. It also has safety features such as pressure sensors and automatic shut-off to ensure safe cooking.

So, while both a pressure cooker and an Instant Pot use pressure cooking technology to cook food quickly and efficiently, an Instant Pot is a multi-functional appliance that offers a wider range of cooking options and more precise control over the cooking process.

Tips for Using The Instant Pot

By following these tips, you can use your instant pot to create delicious, healthy meals with ease.

Start with simple recipes: If you are new to instant pot cooking, start with simple recipes. Once you have mastered the basics, you can move on to more complex dishes.

Use enough liquid: The instant pot requires liquid to create steam and build pressure. Make sure to use enough liquid for your recipe to prevent the pot from burning or giving an error message.

Use the right amount of food: Do not overload the instant pot. It's important to use the right amount of food for your recipe, as too much food can cause the pot to overflow or burn.

Use the correct pressure release method: Depending on your recipe, you may need to use a quick release or natural release method. Make sure to follow the instructions carefully to avoid injury and ensure your food turns out correctly.

Clean the instant pot properly: After using the instant pot, make sure to clean it properly. This will ensure that it lasts longer and functions properly.

The Correct Pressure Release Method for Instant Pot

There are two main methods for pressure release on an Instant Pot: natural release and quick release.

Natural release means allowing the Instant Pot to release pressure on its own without any intervention. This is typically used for recipes with longer cook times and larger volumes of food. To do a natural release, simply turn off the Instant Pot and let it sit for the recommended amount of time in the recipe (usually 10-20 minutes).

Quick release, on the other hand, involves manually releasing the pressure by turning the release valve to the venting position. This is typically used for recipes with shorter cook times and smaller volumes of food. To do a quick release, use a long utensil to turn the pressure release valve to the venting position and allow the steam to escape until the float valve drops.

It's important to always follow the recipe's recommended pressure release method to ensure that your food is cooked properly and safely. Additionally, never attempt to open the Instant Pot while it is still under pressure, as this can be dangerous.

Measurement Conversions

BASIC KITCHEN CONVERSIONS & EQUIVALENTS

DRY MEASUREMENTS CONVERSION CHART

3 TEASPOONS = 1 TABLESPOON = 1/16 CUP

6 TEASPOONS = 2 TABLESPOONS = 1/8 CUP

12 TEASPOONS = 4 TABLESPOONS = 1/4 CUP

24 TEASPOONS = 8 TABLESPOONS = 1/2 CUP

36 TEASPOONS = 12 TABLESPOONS = 3/4 CUP

48 TEASPOONS = 16 TABLESPOONS = 1 CUP

METRIC TO US COOKING CONVERSIONS

OVEN TEMPERATURES

120 °C = 250 °F

160 °C = 320 °F

180° C = 350 °F

205 °C = 400 °F

220 °C = 425 °F

LIQUID MEASUREMENTS CONVERSION CHART

8 FLUID OUNCES = 1 CUP = 1/2 PINT = 1/4 QUART

16 FLUID OUNCES = 2 CUPS = 1 PINT = 1/2 QUART

32 FLUID OUNCES = 4 CUPS = 2 PINTS = 1 QUART

 = 1/4 GALLON

128 FLUID OUNCES = 16 CUPS = 8 PINTS = 4 QUARTS = 1 GALLON

BAKING IN GRAMS

1 CUP FLOUR = 140 GRAMS

1 CUP SUGAR = 150 GRAMS

1 CUP POWDERED SUGAR = 160 GRAMS

1 CUP HEAVY CREAM = 235 GRAMS

VOLUME

1 MILLILITER = 1/5 TEASPOON

5 ML = 1 TEASPOON

15 ML = 1 TABLESPOON

240 ML = 1 CUP OR 8 FLUID OUNCES

1 LITER = 34 FL. OUNCES

WEIGHT

1 GRAM = .035 OUNCES

100 GRAMS = 3.5 OUNCES

500 GRAMS = 1.1 POUNDS

1 KILOGRAM = 35 OUNCES

US TO METRIC COOKING CONVERSIONS

1/5 TSP = 1 ML

1 TSP = 5 ML

1 TBSP = 15 ML

1 FL OUNCE = 30 ML

1 CUP = 237 ML

1 PINT (2 CUPS) = 473 ML

1 QUART (4 CUPS) = .95 LITER

1 GALLON (16 CUPS) = 3.8 LITERS

1 OZ = 28 GRAMS

1 POUND = 454 GRAMS

BUTTER

1 CUP BUTTER = 2 STICKS = 8 OUNCES = 230 GRAMS = 8 TABLESPOONS

WHAT DOES 1 CUP EQUAL

1 CUP = 8 FLUID OUNCES

1 CUP = 16 TABLESPOONS

1 CUP = 48 TEASPOONS

1 CUP = 1/2 PINT

1 CUP = 1/4 QUART

1 CUP = 1/16 GALLON

1 CUP = 240 ML

BAKING PAN CONVERSIONS

1 CUP ALL-PURPOSE FLOUR = 4.5 OZ

1 CUP ROLLED OATS = 3 OZ 1 LARGE EGG = 1.7 OZ

1 CUP BUTTER = 8 OZ 1 CUP MILK = 8 OZ

1 CUP HEAVY CREAM = 8.4 OZ

1 CUP GRANULATED SUGAR = 7.1 OZ

1 CUP PACKED BROWN SUGAR = 7.75 OZ

1 CUP VEGETABLE OIL = 7.7 OZ

1 CUP UNSIFTED POWDERED SUGAR = 4.4 OZ

BAKING PAN CONVERSIONS

9-INCH ROUND CAKE PAN = 12 CUPS

10-INCH TUBE PAN =16 CUPS

11-INCH BUNDT PAN = 12 CUPS

9-INCH SPRINGFORM PAN = 10 CUPS

9 X 5 INCH LOAF PAN = 8 CUPS

9-INCH SQUARE PAN = 8 CUPS

Chapter 2 Breakfast

Chapter 2 Breakfast

Lemony Pancake Bites With Blueberry Syrup

Servings:4 | Cooking Time: 24 Minutes

Ingredients:
- 1 packet Hungry Jack buttermilk pancake mix
- ⅔ cup whole milk
- Juice and zest of ½ medium lemon
- ⅛ teaspoon salt
- 1 cup water
- ½ cup blueberry syrup

Directions:
1. Grease a seven-hole silicone egg mold.
2. In a medium bowl, combine pancake mix, milk, lemon juice and zest, and salt. Fill egg mold with half of batter.
3. Add water to the Instant Pot and insert steam rack. Place filled egg mold on steam rack. Lock lid.
4. Press the Manual or Pressure Cook button and adjust time to 12 minutes. When timer beeps, quick-release pressure until float valve drops. Unlock lid.
5. Allow pancake bites to cool, about 3 minutes until cool enough to handle. Pop out of mold. Repeat with remaining batter.
6. Serve warm with syrup for dipping.

Greek Yogurt With Honey & Walnuts

Servings: 10 | Cooking Time: 15hr

Ingredients:
- 2 tbsp Greek yogurt
- 8 cups milk
- ¼ cup sugar honey
- 1 tsp vanilla extract
- 1 cup walnuts, chopped

Directions:
1. Add the milk to your Instant Pot. Seal the lid and press Yogurt until the display shows "Boil". When the cooking cycle is over, the display will show Yogurt.

Open the lid and check that milk temperature is at least 175°F. Get rid of the skin lying on the milk's surface. Let cool in an ice bath until it becomes warm to the touch.
2. In a bowl, mix one cup of milk and yogurt to make a smooth consistency. Mix the milk with yogurt mixture. Transfer to the pot and place on your Pressure cooker.
3. Seal the lid, press Yogurt, and adjust the timer to 9 hrs. Once cooking is complete, strain the yogurt into a bowl using a strainer with cheesecloth. Chill for 4 hours.
4. Add in vanilla and honey and gently stir well. Spoon the yogurt into glass jars. Serve sprinkled with walnuts and enjoy.

Tomato Mozzarella Basil Egg Bites

Servings:6 | Cooking Time: 8 Minutes

Ingredients:
- 4 large eggs
- 2 tablespoons grated yellow onion
- ½ teaspoon salt
- ½ teaspoon ground black pepper
- 6 cherry tomatoes, quartered
- ¼ cup grated mozzarella cheese
- 2 tablespoons chopped fresh basil
- 1 cup water

Directions:
1. Grease six silicone cupcake liners.
2. In a medium bowl, whisk together eggs, onion, salt, and pepper. Distribute egg mixture evenly among cupcake liners. Add tomatoes, cheese, and basil to each cup.
3. Add water to the Instant Pot and insert steam rack. Place steamer basket on steam rack. Carefully place cupcake liners in basket. Lock lid.
4. Press the Manual or Pressure Cook button and adjust time to 8 minutes. When timer beeps, quick-release pressure until float valve drops. Unlock lid.
5. Remove egg bites. Serve warm.

13 | Instant Pot Cookbook

Chocolate Banana French Toast Casserole

Servings:4 | Cooking Time: 20 Minutes

Ingredients:
- 4 cups cubed bread, dried out overnight, divided
- 2 bananas, peeled and sliced
- 4 tablespoons chocolate syrup, divided
- 2 cups whole milk
- 3 large eggs
- 1 teaspoon vanilla extract
- ¼ cup pure maple syrup
- Pinch of ground nutmeg
- Pinch of sea salt
- 3 tablespoons butter, cut into 3 pats
- 1 cup water

Directions:
1. Grease a 7-cup glass dish. Add 2 cups bread. Arrange banana slices in an even layer over bread. Drizzle 2 tablespoons chocolate syrup over bananas. Add remaining 2 cups bread. Set aside.
2. In a medium bowl, whisk together milk, eggs, vanilla, maple syrup, nutmeg, and salt. Pour over bread; place pats of butter on top.
3. Pour water into Instant Pot. Set trivet in Instant Pot. Place glass dish on top of trivet. Lock lid.
4. Press the Manual button and adjust time to 20 minutes. When the timer beeps, quick-release pressure until float valve drops and then unlock lid.
5. Remove glass bowl from the Instant Pot. Transfer to a rack until cooled. Top with remaining 2 tablespoons chocolate. Serve warm.

Sweet Potato Morning Hash

Servings:4 | Cooking Time: 10 Minutes

Ingredients:
- 6 large eggs
- 1 tablespoon Italian seasoning
- ½ teaspoon sea salt
- ½ teaspoon ground black pepper
- ½ pound ground pork sausage
- 1 large sweet potato, peeled and cubed
- 1 small onion, peeled and diced
- 2 cloves garlic, minced
- 1 medium green bell pepper, seeded and diced
- 2 cups water

Directions:

1. In a medium bowl, whisk together eggs, Italian seasoning, salt, and pepper. Set aside.
2. Press the Sauté button on Instant Pot. Stir-fry sausage, sweet potato, onion, garlic, and bell pepper for 3–5 minutes until onions are translucent.
3. Transfer mixture to a 7-cup greased glass dish. Pour whisked eggs over the sausage mixture.
4. Place trivet in Instant Pot. Pour in water. Place dish with egg mixture onto trivet. Lock lid.
5. Press the Manual button and adjust time to 5 minutes. When timer beeps, quick-release pressure until float valve drops and then unlock lid. Remove dish from Instant Pot. Let sit at room temperature for 5–10 minutes to allow the eggs to set. Slice and serve.

Blueberry-oat Muffins

Servings:6 | Cooking Time: 9 Minutes

Ingredients:
- 1 cup all-purpose baking flour
- ¼ cup old-fashioned oats
- 2 teaspoons baking powder
- ½ teaspoon baking soda
- ⅛ teaspoon salt
- ½ teaspoon vanilla extract
- 3 tablespoons unsalted butter, melted
- 2 large eggs
- 4 tablespoons granulated sugar
- ⅓ cup blueberries
- 1 cup water

Directions:
1. Grease six silicone cupcake liners.
2. In a large bowl, combine flour, oats, baking powder, baking soda, and salt.
3. In a medium bowl, combine vanilla, butter, eggs, and sugar.
4. Pour wet ingredients from medium bowl into the bowl with dry ingredients. Gently combine ingredients. Do not overmix. Fold in blueberries, then spoon mixture into prepared cupcake liners.
5. Add water to the Instant Pot and insert steam rack. Place cupcake liners on top. Lock lid.
6. Press the Manual or Pressure Cook button and adjust time to 9 minutes. When timer beeps, quick-release pressure until float valve drops. Unlock lid.
7. Remove muffins from pot and set aside to cool 30 minutes. Serve.

Cinnamon Roll Doughnut Holes

Servings:14 | Cooking Time: 16 Minutes

Ingredients:
- 1 package Krusteaz Cinnamon Roll Supreme Mix (includes icing packet)
- 6 tablespoons unsalted butter, melted
- ½ cup cold water
- ¼ cup chopped pecans
- 1 cup water

Directions:
1. In a medium bowl, combine dry mix, butter, and ½ cup cold water. Fold in pecans. Spoon half of batter into a greased seven-hole silicone egg mold. If your egg mold has a silicone top, use this. If your egg mold came with a plastic top, do not use. Instead, cover with aluminum foil.
2. Add 1 cup water to the Instant Pot and insert steam rack. Place egg mold on steam rack. Lock lid.
3. Press the Manual or Pressure Cook button and adjust time to 8 minutes. When timer beeps, quick-release pressure until float valve drops. Unlock lid.
4. Pop doughnut holes out of egg mold and repeat with remaining batter.
5. When doughnut holes are cooled, mix icing packet with 1 ½ tablespoons water and dip doughnut holes into glaze to cover. Serve.

Peanut Butter And Banana Oatmeal

Servings:2 | Cooking Time: 7 Minutes

Ingredients:
- 1 cup old-fashioned oats
- 1 ¼ cups water
- 1 large ripe banana, peeled and mashed
- 1 tablespoon packed light brown sugar
- ¼ teaspoon vanilla extract
- ¼ teaspoon ground cinnamon
- ⅛ teaspoon salt
- 2 tablespoons crunchy peanut butter

Directions:
1. In the Instant Pot, add oats, water, banana, brown sugar, vanilla, cinnamon, and salt. Stir to combine. Lock lid.
2. Press the Manual or Pressure Cook button and adjust time to 7 minutes. When timer beeps, let pressure release naturally until float valve drops. Unlock lid.
3. Stir in peanut butter, then spoon oatmeal into two bowls. Serve warm.

Light & Fruity Yogurt

Servings: 12 | Cooking Time: 24hr

Ingredients:
- ¼ cup Greek yogurt containing active cultures
- 1 lb raspberries, mashed
- 1 cup sugar
- 3 tbsp gelatin
- 1 tbsp fresh orange juice
- 8 cups milk

Directions:
1. In a bowl, add sugar and raspberries and stir well to dissolve the sugar. Let sit for 30 minutes at room temperature. Add in orange juice and gelatin and mix well until dissolved. Remove the mixture and place in a sealable container, close, and allow to sit for 12 hrs to 24 hrs at room temperature before placing in the fridge. Refrigerate for a maximum of 2 weeks.
2. Into the cooker, add milk, and close the lid. The steam vent should be set to Venting then to Sealing. Select Yogurt until "Boil" is showed on display. When complete, there will be a display of "Yogurt" on the screen.
3. Open the lid and using a food thermometer, ensure the milk temperature is at least 185°F. Transfer the steel pot to a wire rack and allow to cool for 30 minutes until the milk has reached 110°F.
4. In a bowl, mix ½ cup warm milk and yogurt. Transfer the mixture into the remaining warm milk and stir without having to scrape the steel pot's bottom. Take the steel pot back to the base of the pot and seal the lid.
5. Select Yogurt and cook for 8 hrs. Allow the yogurt to chill in a refrigerator for 1-2 hrs. Transfer the chilled yogurt to a bowl and stir in fresh raspberry jam.

Pumpkin Steel Cut Oats With Cinnamon

Servings: 4 | Cooking Time: 25 Minutes

Ingredients:
- 1 tbsp butter
- 2 cups steel-cut oats
- ¼ tsp cinnamon
- 1 cup pumpkin puree
- 3 tbsp maple syrup
- 2 tsp pumpkin seeds, toasted

Directions:
1. Melt butter on Sauté. Add in cinnamon, oats, pumpkin puree, and 3 cups of water. Seal the lid, select Porridge and cook for 10 minutes on High Pressure to get a few bite oats or for 14 minutes to form soft oats. Do a quick release. Open the lid and stir in maple syrup. Top with pumpkin seeds and serve.

Grandma's Country Gravy

Servings:6 | Cooking Time: 16 Minutes

Ingredients:
- 2 tablespoons unsalted butter
- 1 pound ground pork sausage
- 1 small sweet onion, peeled and diced
- ¼ cup chicken broth
- ¼ cup all-purpose flour
- 1 ½ cups heavy cream
- ½ teaspoon salt
- 1 tablespoon ground black pepper

Directions:
1. Press the Sauté button on the Instant Pot. Add butter and heat until melted. Add sausage and onion and stir-fry 3–5 minutes until onions are translucent. The pork will still be a little pink in places. Add broth. Press the Cancel button. Lock lid.
2. Press the Manual or Pressure Cook button and adjust time to 1 minute. When timer beeps, quick-release pressure until float valve drops. Unlock lid. Whisk in flour, cream, salt, and pepper.
3. Press the Keep Warm button and let the gravy sit about 5–10 minutes to allow to thicken. Remove from heat. Serve warm.

Banana Nut Bread Oatmeal

Servings:2 | Cooking Time: 7 Minutes

Ingredients:
- 1 cup old-fashioned oats
- 1 cup water
- 1 cup whole milk
- 2 ripe bananas, peeled and sliced
- 2 tablespoons pure maple syrup
- 2 teaspoons ground cinnamon
- ¼ teaspoon vanilla extract
- 2 tablespoons chopped walnuts
- Pinch of salt

Directions:
1. In the Instant Pot bowl, add the oats, water, milk, bananas, maple syrup, cinnamon, vanilla, walnuts, and salt. Stir to combine. Lock lid.
2. Press the Manual button and adjust time to 7 minutes. When the timer beeps, let pressure release naturally until float valve drops and then unlock lid.
3. Stir oatmeal. Spoon the cooked oats into two bowls. Serve warm.

Maple French Toast Casserole

Servings:4 | Cooking Time: 20 Minutes

Ingredients:
- 4 cups cubed French bread
- 1 cup whole milk
- 3 large eggs
- 1 tablespoon granulated sugar
- 1 teaspoon vanilla extract
- ¼ cup pure maple syrup
- ⅛ teaspoon salt
- 3 tablespoons unsalted butter, cut into 3 pats
- 1 cup water

Directions:
1. Grease a 7-cup glass baking dish. Add bread. Set aside.
2. In a medium bowl, whisk together milk, eggs, sugar, vanilla, maple syrup, and salt. Pour over bread; place butter pats on top.
3. Add water to the Instant Pot and insert steam rack. Place glass baking dish on top of steam rack. Lock lid.
4. Press the Manual or Pressure Cook button and adjust time to 20 minutes. When timer beeps, quick-release pressure until float valve drops. Unlock lid.
5. Remove bowl and transfer to a cooling rack until set, about 20 minutes. Serve.

Crustless Crab Quiche

Servings:6 | Cooking Time: 10 Minutes

Ingredients:

- 6 large eggs
- ¼ cup unsweetened almond milk
- 2 teaspoons fresh thyme leaves
- ½ teaspoon sea salt
- ¼ teaspoon ground black pepper
- ½ teaspoon hot sauce
- ½ pound crabmeat
- ¼ cup crumbled goat cheese
- 2 thick slices bacon, diced
- ¼ cup peeled and diced onion
- ¼ cup seeded and diced green bell pepper
- 2 cups water

Directions:

1. In a medium bowl, whisk eggs, milk, thyme leaves, salt, pepper, and hot sauce. Stir in crabmeat and goat cheese. Set aside.
2. Grease a 7-cup glass dish. Set aside.
3. Press the Sauté button on Instant Pot. Add diced bacon and brown for 2 minutes, rendering some fat. Add onion and bell pepper and stir-fry with bacon until tender. Transfer mixture to the glass container. Pour in egg mixture.
4. Place trivet in Instant Pot. Pour in water. Place dish with egg mixture onto trivet. Lock lid.
5. Press the Manual button and adjust time to 5 minutes. When timer beeps, let pressure release naturally for 10 minutes. Quick-release any additional pressure until float valve drops and then unlock lid.
6. Remove dish from Instant Pot. Let cool for 10 minutes to allow eggs to set. Slice and serve.

Pimiento Cheese Grits

Servings:4 | Cooking Time: 10 Minutes

Ingredients:

- ¾ cup plus 1 ½ cups water, divided
- 1 cup stone-ground grits
- 2 tablespoons unsalted butter
- 1 teaspoon salt
- ½ teaspoon ground black pepper
- ½ cup grated sharp Cheddar cheese
- 1 jar diced pimientos, drained

Directions:

1. Add ¾ cup water to the Instant Pot and insert steam rack.
2. In a 7-cup glass baking dish that fits down into the pot insert, combine grits, butter, remaining 1 ½ cups water, salt, and pepper. Lock lid.
3. Press the Rice button. When timer beeps, quick-release pressure until float valve drops. Unlock lid.
4. Stir in cheese and pimientos. Serve warm.

Buckwheat Pancake With Yogurt & Berries

Servings: 4 | Cooking Time: 15 Minutes

Ingredients:

- 1 cup buckwheat flour
- 2 tsp baking powder
- 1 ¼ cups milk
- 1 egg
- 1 tsp vanilla sugar
- 1 tsp strawberry extract
- 1 cup Greek yogurt
- 1 cup fresh berries

Directions:

1. In a bowl, whisk milk and egg until foamy. Gradually add flour and continue to beat until combined. Add baking powder, strawberry extract, and vanilla sugar. Spoon the batter in a greased cake pan. Pour 1 cup of water into the pot. Place a trivet. Lay the pan on the trivet. Seal the lid and cook for 5 minutes on High Pressure. Do a quick release. Top pancake with yogurt and berries.

Pumpkin Muffins

Servings:6 | Cooking Time: 9 Minutes

Ingredients:
- 1 ¼ cups all-purpose flour
- 2 teaspoons baking powder
- ½ teaspoon baking soda
- 1 teaspoon pumpkin pie spice
- ⅛ teaspoon salt
- ¼ cup pumpkin purée
- ½ teaspoon vanilla extract
- 1 tablespoon unsalted butter, melted
- 2 large eggs
- ⅓ cup packed light brown sugar
- 1 cup water

Directions:
1. Grease six silicone cupcake liners.
2. In a large bowl, combine flour, baking powder, baking soda, pumpkin pie spice, and salt.
3. In a medium bowl, combine pumpkin purée, vanilla, butter, eggs, and brown sugar.
4. Pour wet ingredients from medium bowl into large bowl with dry ingredients. Gently combine ingredients. Do not overmix. Spoon mixture into prepared cupcake liners.
5. Add water to the Instant Pot and insert steam rack. Place cupcake liners on top. Lock lid.
6. Press the Manual or Pressure Cook button and adjust time to 9 minutes. When timer beeps, quick-release pressure until float valve drops. Unlock lid.
7. Remove muffins from pot and set aside to cool 30 minutes. Serve.

Banana & Vanilla Pancakes

Servings: 6 | Cooking Time: 15 Minutes

Ingredients:
- 2 bananas, mashed
- 1 ¼ cups milk
- 2 eggs
- 1 ½ cups rolled oats
- 1 ½ tsp baking powder
- 1 tsp vanilla extract
- 2 tsp coconut oil
- 1 tbsp honey

Directions:
1. Combine the bananas, milk, eggs, oats, baking powder, vanilla, coconut oil, and honey in a blender and pulse until a completely smooth batter. Grease the inner pot with cooking spray. Spread 1 spoon batter at the bottom. Cook for 2 minutes on Sauté, flip the crepe, and cook for another minute. Repeat the process with the remaining batter. Serve immediately with your favorite topping.

Pumpkin Spice Latte French Toast Casserole

Servings:4 | Cooking Time: 20 Minutes

Ingredients:
- 4 cups cubed whole-wheat bread
- 1½ cups whole milk
- ¼ cup brewed coffee, cooled
- 3 large eggs
- ¼ cup pumpkin purée
- 1 teaspoon vanilla extract
- ¼ cup pure maple syrup
- 2 teaspoons pumpkin pie spice
- Pinch of sea salt
- 3 tablespoons butter, cut into 3 pats
- 1 cup water

Directions:
1. Grease a 7-cup glass dish. Add bread. Set aside.
2. In a medium bowl, whisk together milk, coffee, eggs, pumpkin purée, vanilla, maple syrup, pumpkin pie spice, and salt. Pour over bread; place pats of butter on top.
3. Pour water into Instant Pot. Set trivet in Instant Pot. Place glass dish on top of trivet. Lock lid.
4. Press the Manual button and adjust time to 20 minutes. When the timer beeps, quick-release the pressure until float valve drops and then unlock lid.
5. Remove glass bowl from the Instant Pot. Transfer to a rack until cool. Serve.

Pecan Chocolate Chip Breakfast Oats

Servings:2 | Cooking Time: 7 Minutes

Ingredients:
- 1 cup old-fashioned oats
- 1 cup water
- 1 cup whole milk
- ¼ teaspoon vanilla extract
- 2 tablespoons packed light brown sugar
- 2 tablespoons chopped pecans
- ⅛ teaspoon salt
- 2 tablespoons mini chocolate chips

Directions:
1. In the Instant Pot, add oats, water, milk, vanilla, brown sugar, pecans, and salt. Stir to combine. Lock lid.
2. Press the Manual or Pressure Cook button and adjust time to 7 minutes. When timer beeps, quick-release pressure until float valve drops. Unlock lid.
3. Stir oatmeal, then spoon into two bowls and garnish with chocolate chips. Serve warm.

Georgia Peach French Toast Casserole

Servings:4 | Cooking Time: 20 Minutes

Ingredients:
- 4 cups cubed French bread, dried out overnight
- 2 cups diced, peeled ripe peaches
- 1 cup whole milk
- 3 large eggs
- 1 teaspoon vanilla extract
- ¼ cup granulated sugar
- ⅛ teaspoon salt
- 3 tablespoons unsalted butter, cut into 3 pats
- 1 cup water

Directions:
1. Grease a 7-cup glass baking dish. Add bread to dish in an even layer. Add peaches in an even layer over bread. Set aside.
2. In a medium bowl, whisk together milk, eggs, vanilla, sugar, and salt. Pour over bread; place butter pats on top.
3. Add water to the Instant Pot and insert steam rack. Place glass baking dish on top of steam rack. Lock lid.
4. Press the Manual or Pressure Cook button and adjust time to 20 minutes. When timer beeps, quick-release pressure until float valve drops. Unlock lid.
5. Remove bowl and transfer to a cooling rack until set, about 20 minutes. Serve.

Speedy Soft-boiled Eggs

Servings: 4 | Cooking Time: 10 Minutes

Ingredients:
- 4 large eggs
- Salt and pepper to taste

Directions:
1. To the pressure cooker, add 1 cup of water and place a wire rack. Place eggs on it. Seal the lid, press Steam, and cook for 3 minutes on High Pressure. Do a quick release.
2. Allow to cool in an ice bath. Peel the eggs and season with salt and pepper before serving.

Brunchy Sausage Bowl

Servings:4 | Cooking Time: 10 Minutes

Ingredients:
- 1 pound pork sausage links
- 2 large potatoes, peeled and thinly sliced
- 1 medium red bell pepper, seeded and diced
- 1 medium sweet onion, peeled and diced
- 1 can creamed corn
- ½ teaspoon sea salt
- ¼ teaspoon ground black pepper
- ¾ cup tomato juice

Directions:
1. Press the Sauté button on Instant Pot. Add sausage links and brown for 4–5 minutes. Move the sausages to a plate.
2. Layer the potatoes, bell pepper, onion, and corn in the Instant Pot. Sprinkle with salt and pepper. Place sausage links on top of the corn. Pour the tomato juice over the top of the other ingredients in the Instant Pot. Lock lid.
3. Press the Manual button and adjust time to 5 minutes. When the timer beeps, let the pressure release naturally for at least 10 minutes.
4. Quick-release any additional pressure until the float valve drops and then unlock lid. Serve warm.

Sunday Brunch Sausage Gravy

Servings:10 | Cooking Time: 10 Minutes

Ingredients:
- 2 tablespoons butter
- 1 pound ground pork sausage
- 1 small sweet onion, peeled and diced
- ¼ cup chicken broth
- ¼ cup all-purpose flour
- 1½ cups heavy cream
- ½ teaspoon sea salt
- 1 tablespoon ground black pepper

Directions:
1. Press the Sauté button on the Instant Pot. Add butter and heat until melted. Add pork sausage and onion. Stir-fry 3–5 minutes until onions are translucent. The pork will still be a little pink in places. Add chicken broth. Lock lid.
2. Press the Manual button and adjust time to 1 minute. When the timer beeps, quick-release the pressure until the float valve drops and then unlock the lid. Whisk in flour, cream, salt, and pepper.
3. Press the Keep Warm button and let the gravy sit for about 5–10 minutes to allow the sauce to thicken. Remove from heat and serve warm.

Spinach & Feta Pie With Cherry Tomatoes

Servings: 2 | Cooking Time: 35 Minutes

Ingredients:
- 4 eggs
- Salt and pepper to taste
- ½ cup heavy cream
- 1 cup cherry tomatoes, halved
- 1 cup baby spinach
- 1 spring onion, chopped
- ¼ cup feta, crumbled
- 1 tbsp parsley, chopped

Directions:
1. Grease a baking dish with cooking spray and add in the spinach and onion. In a bowl, whisk the eggs, heavy cream, salt, and pepper. Pour over the spinach and arrange the cherry tomato on top. Sprinkle with the feta.
2. Add a cup of water to the Instant Pot and insert a trivet. Place the dish on the trivet. Seal the lid, press Manual, and cook on High pressure for 15 minutes.

Release pressure naturally for 10 minutes. Scatter parsley to serve.

Bacon Onion Cheddar Frittata

Servings:4 | Cooking Time: 12 Minutes

Ingredients:
- 6 large eggs
- 2 teaspoons Italian seasoning
- ½ cup shredded Cheddar cheese
- ½ teaspoon salt
- ¼ teaspoon ground black pepper
- 1 tablespoon olive oil
- 4 slices bacon, diced
- 1 small yellow onion, peeled and diced
- 1 cup water

Directions:
1. In a medium bowl, whisk together eggs, Italian seasoning, cheese, salt, and pepper. Set aside.
2. Press the Sauté button on the Instant Pot and heat oil. Add bacon and onion and stir-fry 3–4 minutes until onions are translucent and bacon is almost crisp. Press the Cancel button.
3. Transfer cooked mixture to a greased 7-cup glass bowl and set aside to cool 5 minutes. Pour whisked egg mixture over the cooked mixture and stir to combine.
4. Add water to the Instant Pot and insert steam rack. Place glass bowl with egg mixture on steam rack. Lock lid.
5. Press the Manual or Pressure Cook button and adjust time to 8 minutes. When timer beeps, let pressure release naturally until float valve drops. Unlock lid.
6. Remove bowl from pot and let sit 10 minutes to allow eggs to set. Slice and serve warm.

Honey Butternut Squash Cake Oatmeal

Servings: 4 | Cooking Time: 35 Minutes

Ingredients:
- 3 ½ cups coconut milk
- 1 cup steel-cut oats
- 8 oz butternut squash, grated
- ½ cup sultanas
- 1/3 cup honey
- ¾ tsp ground ginger
- ½ tsp salt
- ½ tsp orange zest
- ¼ tsp ground nutmeg
- ¼ cup walnuts, chopped
- ½ tsp vanilla extract
- ½ tsp sugar

Directions:
1. In the cooker, mix sultanas, orange zest, ginger, milk, honey, butternut squash, salt, oats, and nutmeg. Seal the lid and cook on High Pressure for 12 minutes. Do a natural release for 10 minutes. Into the oatmeal, stir in the vanilla extract and sugar. Top with walnuts and serve.

Nutty Steel-cut Oats

Servings:2 | Cooking Time: 12 Minutes

Ingredients:
- 1 ½ cups steel-cut oats
- 2 cups water
- 1 cup whole milk
- ½ teaspoon vanilla extract
- 2 tablespoons packed light brown sugar
- 2 tablespoons chopped walnuts
- ⅛ teaspoon salt

Directions:
1. In the Instant Pot, add oats, water, milk, vanilla, brown sugar, walnuts, and salt. Stir to combine. Lock lid.
2. Press the Manual or Pressure Cook button and adjust time to 12 minutes. When timer beeps, quick-release pressure until float valve drops. Unlock lid.
3. Stir oatmeal, then spoon into two bowls. Serve warm.

Walnut & Pumpkin Strudel

Servings: 8 | Cooking Time: 55 Minutes

Ingredients:
- 2 cups pumpkin puree
- 1 tsp vanilla extract
- 2 cups Greek yogurt
- 2 eggs
- 2 tbsp brown sugar
- 2 tbsp butter, softened
- 2 puff pastry sheets
- 1 cup walnuts, chopped

Directions:
1. In a bowl, mix butter, yogurt, and vanilla until smooth. Unfold the pastry and cut each sheet into 4-inch x 7-inch pieces; brush with some beaten eggs. Place approximately 2 tbsp of pumpkin puree, sugar, and 2 tbsp of the yogurt mixture at the middle of each pastry, sprinkle with walnuts. Fold the sheets and brush with the remaining eggs.
2. Cut the surface with a sharp knife and gently place each strudel into an oiled baking dish. Pour 1 cup of water into the pot and insert the trivet. Place the pan on top. Seal the lid and cook for 25 minutes on High Pressure. Release the pressure naturally for about 10 minutes. Let it chill for 10 minutes. Serve.

Breakfast Frittata

Servings: 4 | Cooking Time: 25 Minutes

Ingredients:
- 8 beaten eggs
- 1 cup cherry tomatoes, halved
- 1 tbsp Dijon mustard
- 1 cup mushrooms, chopped
- Salt and pepper to taste
- 1 cup sharp cheddar, grated

Directions:
1. Combine the eggs, mushrooms, mustard, salt, pepper, and ½ cup of cheddar cheese in a bowl. Pour in a greased baking pan and top with the remaining cheddar cheese and cherry tomatoes. Add 1 cup of water to your Instant Pot and fit in a trivet. Place the baking pan on the trivet.
2. Seal the lid. Select Manual and cook for 15 minutes on High. When ready, perform a quick pressure release and unlock the lid. Slice into wedges before serving.

Chapter 3 Appetizers, Soups & Sides

Authentic German Salad With Bacon

Servings: 6 | Cooking Time: 20 Minutes

Ingredients:
- 6 smoked bacon slices, chopped
- 6 red potatoes, peeled and quartered
- ½ cup apple cider vinegar
- 2 tsp mustard
- Salt and pepper to serve
- 2 red onions, chopped

Directions:
1. Set your Instant Pot to Sauté. Briefly brown the bacon for 5 minutes until crispy. Set aside. In a bowl, mix mustard, vinegar, ½ cup water, salt, and pepper. In the pot, add potatoes, bacon, and onions and top with the vinegar mixture. Seal the lid and cook for 6 minutes on High Pressure. Release pressure naturally for 10 minutes. Transfer to a serving plate. Enjoy!

Garlic & Herbed Potatoes

Servings: 4 | Cooking Time: 25 Minutes

Ingredients:
- 1 ½ lb potatoes
- 3 tbsp butter
- 3 cloves garlic, chopped
- 2 tbsp rosemary, chopped
- ½ tsp fresh thyme, chopped
- ½ tsp parsley, chopped
- Salt and pepper to taste
- ½ cup vegetable broth

Directions:
1. Use a small knife to pierce each potato to ensure there are no blowouts when placed under pressure. Melt butter on Sauté. Add in potatoes, rosemary, parsley, pepper, salt, thyme, and garlic, and cook for 10 minutes until potatoes are browned and the mixture is aromatic. Stir in the broth. Seal the lid and cook for 5 minutes on High Pressure. Release the pressure quickly. Serve and enjoy!

Delicious Broccoli & Cauliflower Salad

Servings: 4 | Cooking Time: 10 Minutes

Ingredients:
- 1 lb cauliflower florets
- 1 lb broccoli, into florets
- 3 garlic cloves, crushed
- ¼ tbsp olive oil
- 1 tsp salt
- 1 tbsp dry rosemary

Directions:
1. Cut the veggies into bite-sized pieces and place them in the pot. Add olive oil and 1 cup of water. Season with salt, garlic, and rosemary. Seal the lid. Cook on High Pressure for 3 minutes. When ready, do a quick release.

Pecorino Mushroom Soup

Servings: 4 | Cooking Time: 30 Minutes

Ingredients:
- 2 cups Pecorino, grated
- 3 cups Mushrooms, chopped
- 2 tbsp Butter
- 1 onion, chopped
- 2 Garlic cloves, minced
- 2 cups Thyme, chopped
- 2 tbsp Almond flour
- 3 cups Chicken stock

Directions:
1. Place the butter and onion in your Instant Pot and cook for 2 minutes on Sauté. Mix in mushrooms, garlic cloves, thyme, chicken stock, and almond flour. Seal the lid, select Manual, and cook for 10 minutes on High. When done, allow a natural release for 10 minutes. Serve garnished with grated Pecorino cheese.

Weekend Beef Balls

Servings: 4 | Cooking Time: 20 Minutes

Ingredients:
- 1 lb ground beef
- 2 tbsp milk
- 2 tbsp oil
- 1 tbsp Italian seasoning
- 1 onion, chopped
- 2 eggs
- 2 wheat bread slices
- Salt and pepper to taste

Directions:
1. Place two slices of bread in a bowl. Add ¼ cup water and let soak for 5 minutes. Mix beef, milk, oil, Italian seasoning mix, onion, eggs, salt, and pepper.
2. Add soaked bread and shape balls with approximately ¼ cup of the mixture. Flatten each ball with your hands and place it on a lightly floured surface. Heat the oil on Sauté. Add the meatballs and fry for 3 minutes per side. Serve immediately with garlic sauce.

One-pot Sausages With Peppers & Onions

Servings: 4 | Cooking Time: 20 Minutes

Ingredients:
- 2 red bell peppers, cut into strips
- 4 pork sausages
- 1 sweet onion, sliced
- 1 tbsp olive oil
- ½ cup beef broth
- ¼ cup white wine
- 1 tsp garlic, minced
- Salt and pepper to taste

Directions:
1. On Sauté, add the sausages and brown them for a few minutes. Remove to a plate and discard the liquid. Press Cancel. Wipe clean the cooker and heat the oil on Sauté. Stir in onion and bell peppers. Stir-fry them for 5 minutes until soft. Add garlic and cook for a minute. Add the sausages and pour in broth and wine. Season with salt and pepper. Seal the lid and cook for 5 minutes on High pressure. Once done, do a quick pressure release. Serve.

Tangy Egg Snacks

Servings: 6 | Cooking Time: 14 Minutes

Ingredients:
- ¼ tsp onion powder
- 6 eggs
- ½ tsp chili powder
- ¼ tsp sea salt
- ¼ tsp garlic powder
- Salt and black pepper to taste

Directions:
1. Grease a baking dish with cooking spray, crack the eggs, and whisk them. Sprinkle with salt, pepper, onion powder, chili powder, and garlic powder. Pour in 1 cup of water in your Instant Pot and fit in a trivet. Place the dish on the trivet and seal the lid. Select Manual and cook for 4 minutes on High pressure. When done, perform a quick pressure release and unlock the lid. Remove onto a cutting board and slice into cubes before serving.

Steamed Broccoli

Servings:4 | Cooking Time: 0 Minutes (it Will Cook While The Pressure Builds)

Ingredients:
- 1 cup water
- 1 medium head broccoli, chopped
- 1 teaspoon lemon juice
- ½ teaspoon sea salt
- 2 teaspoons ghee

Directions:
1. Pour water into Instant Pot. Insert a steamer basket and arrange broccoli on the basket in an even layer. Lock lid.
2. Press the Steam button and adjust time to 0 minutes. The broccoli will steam in the time it takes the pressure to build. When timer beeps, quick-release pressure until float valve drops and then unlock lid.
3. Use retriever tongs to remove steamer basket. Transfer broccoli to a serving dish and toss with lemon juice, salt, and ghee. Serve warm.

Sausage & Cannellini Bean Stew

Servings: 6 | Cooking Time: 35 Minutes

Ingredients:
- 1 cup cannellini beans
- 2 tbsp olive oil
- 1 lb Italian sausages, halved
- 1 celery stalk, chopped
- 1 carrot, chopped
- 1 onion, chopped
- 1 sprig fresh sage
- 1 sprig fresh rosemary
- 1 bay leaf
- 2 cups vegetable stock
- 3 cups fresh spinach
- 1 tsp salt

Directions:
1. Warm oil on Sauté in your Instant pot. Add in sausage pieces and sear for 5 minutes until browned; set aside on a plate. To the pot, add celery, onion, bay leaf, sage, carrot, salt, and rosemary; cook for 3 minutes to soften slightly. Stir in vegetable stock and beans. Arrange seared sausage on top of the beans. Seal the lid, press Bean/Chili, and cook on High for 10 minutes. Release pressure naturally for 10 minutes. Get rid of bay leaf, rosemary, and sage. Mix in spinach and serve.

Spicy Pumpkin Curry

Servings: 4 | Cooking Time: 30 Minutes

Ingredients:
- 4 spring onions, chopped into lengths
- 1 ½ lb pumpkin, chopped
- 4 cups chicken stock
- ½ cup buttermilk
- 2 tbsp curry powder
- 1 tsp ground turmeric
- ½ tsp ground cumin
- ¼ tsp cayenne pepper
- 2 bay leaves
- Salt and pepper to taste
- 2 tbsp cilantro, chopped

Directions:
1. In the pot, stir in pumpkin, buttermilk, curry, turmeric, spring onions, stock, cumin, and cayenne. Season with pepper and salt. Add bay leaves to the liquid and ensure they are submerged. Seal the lid, press Soup/Broth and cook for 10 minutes on High.

2. Naturally release the pressure for 10 minutes. Discard bay leaves. Transfer the soup to a blender and process until smooth. Use a fine-mesh strainer to strain the soup. Garnish with cilantro before serving.

Asparagus & Mushrooms With Bacon

Servings: 4 | Cooking Time: 30 Minutes

Ingredients:
- 1 lb asparagus, trimmed
- 6 oz bacon, chopped
- 1 clove garlic, minced
- 1 yellow onion, chopped
- 8 oz mushrooms, sliced
- Salt and pepper to taste
- 1 tbsp balsamic vinegar

Directions:
1. Place asparagus in your Instant Pot and pour in water. Seal the lid, select Manual, and cook for 3 minutes on High pressure. When ready, allow a natural release for 10 minutes and unlock the lid. Strain asparagus; set aside.
2. Press Sauté on the pot and add bacon; cook for 1-2 minutes. Stir in garlic and onion and sauté for 2 minutes. Mix in mushrooms and cook until they are soft. Mix in cooked asparagus, salt, pepper, and balsamic vinegar and combine. Serve immediately.

Simple Carrot & Oregano Soup

Servings: 4 | Cooking Time: 30 Minutes

Ingredients:
- 2 carrots, chopped
- 4 cups vegetable broth
- 1 tbsp butter
- ½ tsp dried oregano
- ½ tsp salt

Directions:
1. Add carrots, broth, butter, oregano, and salt to the pot. Seal the lid and cook on Manual/Pressure Cook for 12 minutes on High. Do a natural release for 10 minutes. Transfer to a food processor and pulse until creamy.

Beet & Potato Soup

Servings: 4 | Cooking Time: 45 Minutes

Ingredients:
- 2 tbsp olive oil
- 2 garlic cloves, minced
- 1 carrot, chopped
- 3 potatoes, chopped
- ¾ lb beets, peeled, chopped
- 4 cups vegetable broth
- 1 onion, chopped
- Salt and pepper to taste
- ¼ cup basil leaves, chopped

Directions:
1. Heat the olive oil in your Instant Pot on Sauté. Place the onion, carrot, and garlic paste and cook for 3 minutes. Stir in vegetable broth, beets, and potatoes and seal the lid. Select Manual and cook for 25 minutes.
2. Once ready, allow a natural release for 10 minutes, then perform a quick pressure release and unlock the lid. Blend the soup using an immersion blender and adjust the seasoning. Serve topped with basil.

Twice-baked Potatoes

Servings:4 | Cooking Time: 13 Minutes

Ingredients:
- 1 cup water
- 2 medium russet potatoes
- 2 slices bacon, cooked and crumbled
- ¼ cup whole milk
- 4 tablespoons unsalted butter
- ½ cup shredded Cheddar cheese, divided
- ½ teaspoon salt
- ¼ teaspoon ground black pepper

Directions:
1. Add water to the Instant Pot and insert steamer basket. Pierce potatoes with a fork and add to basket. Lock lid.
2. Press the Manual or Pressure Cook button and adjust time to 10 minutes. When timer beeps, let pressure release naturally until float valve drops. Press the Cancel button. Unlock lid.
3. Transfer potatoes to a cutting board and let cool enough to handle.
4. In a medium mixing bowl, add bacon, milk, butter, ¼ cup cheese, salt and pepper.

5. Slice potatoes in half lengthwise. Scoop out potato flesh, leaving a bowl-like shell.
6. Add scooped potatoes to bowl with remaining ingredients. Using a potato masher or the back of a fork, work ingredients together. Distribute mixture evenly among the bowl-like shells. Sprinkle with remaining cheese. Place potatoes in basket and insert in the Instant Pot. Lock lid.
7. Press the Manual or Pressure Cook button and adjust time to 3 minutes. When timer beeps, let pressure release naturally until float valve drops. Unlock lid. Serve.

Wild Mushroom Soup

Servings:4 | Cooking Time: 25 Minutes

Ingredients:
- 3 tablespoons unsalted butter
- 1 small sweet onion, peeled and diced
- 2 cups sliced mushrooms (shiitake, cremini, portobello, etc.)
- 4 cups chicken broth
- 1 tablespoon Italian seasoning
- 1 teaspoon salt
- ½ teaspoon ground black pepper
- 1 cup heavy cream
- 2 teaspoons cooking sherry

Directions:
1. Press the Sauté button on the Instant Pot. Add butter and heat until melted, then add onion. Sauté 3–5 minutes until onions are translucent.
2. Add mushrooms, broth, Italian seasoning, salt, and pepper. Press the Cancel button. Lock lid.
3. Press the Soup button and adjust time to 20 minutes. When timer beeps, let pressure release naturally for 10 minutes. Quick-release any additional pressure until float valve drops. Unlock lid.
4. Add cream and sherry. Use an immersion blender directly in pot to blend soup until desired consistency is reached, either chunky or smooth.
5. Ladle soup into bowls. Serve warm.

Sumac Red Potatoes

Servings: 4 | Cooking Time: 16 Minutes

Ingredients:
- 2 tbsp butter
- 1 lb red potatoes wedges
- 2 tbsp sumac
- Salt and pepper to taste

Directions:
1. Melt the butter in your Instant Pot on Sauté. Mix the potatoes, sumac, and ½ cup of water and seal the lid. Select Manual and cook for 6 minutes on High pressure. Once ready, perform a quick pressure release and unlock the lid. Sprinkle with salt and pepper. Serve immediately.

Hearty Beef Soup

Servings: 6 | Cooking Time: 65 Minutes

Ingredients:
- 2 tbsp olive oil
- 2 lb beef stew meat, cubed
- 1 leek, finely chopped
- 2 garlic cloves, minced
- 2 carrots, chopped
- 1 celery stalk, chopped
- ½ cup pearl barley
- 1 bay leaf
- 6 cups beef bone broth
- ½ tsp soy sauce sauce
- Salt and pepper to taste
- 1 tbsp Parmesan, grated

Directions:
1. Warm the olive oil in your Instant Pot on Sauté. Season beef with salt and pepper and cook in the pot for 10 minutes, stirring frequently; set aside. Add the leek, garlic, carrots, and celery to the pot and cook for 4 minutes. Put the beef back to the pot with pearl barley, bay leaf, beef broth, and soy sauce. Seal the lid and select Manual.
2. Cook for 30 minutes on High pressure. When done, allow a natural release for 10 minutes, then perform a quick pressure release and unlock the lid. Discard the bay leaf. Adjust the taste and top with Parmesan cheese.

Vegetable & Ground Pork Stew

Servings: 6 | Cooking Time: 30 Minutes

Ingredients:
- 1 ¼ lb ground pork
- 1 cup cabbage, shredded
- ½ cup chopped celery
- 2 red onions, chopped
- 2 large tomatoes, chopped
- 1 carrot, shredded
- 2 cups water
- 1 red bell pepper, chopped
- 1 green bell pepper, diced
- 1 yellow bell pepper, diced
- ¼ tsp cumin
- 1 tsp red pepper flakes
- Salt and pepper to taste
- 2 tbsp cilantro, chopped

Directions:
1. Coat with cooking spray. Add the pork and cook until browned on Sauté, 6 minutes. Stir in cabbage, celery, onions, tomatoes, carrot, water, bell peppers, cumin, red pepper flakes, salt, and black pepper. Seal the lid and set to Pressure Cook for 15 minutes. Do a quick pressure release. Sprinkle with cilantro and serve.

Chicken Broth

Servings:6 | Cooking Time: 30 Minutes

Ingredients:
- 1 chicken carcass from a whole chicken
- 2 large carrots, peeled and cut into chunks
- 2 stalks celery, cut into chunks
- 1 small onion, peeled and chopped
- 1 bay leaf
- 2 cloves garlic, peeled and halved
- ½ teaspoon apple cider vinegar
- 1 teaspoon sea salt
- 6 cups water

Directions:
1. Place all ingredients into the Instant Pot. Press the Manual button and adjust time to 30 minutes. When timer beeps, let pressure release naturally until float valve drops and then unlock lid.
2. Use a slotted spoon to retrieve and discard any large items from the broth. Strain the remaining liquid through a fine sieve or cheesecloth. Refrigerate broth for up to 4 days or freeze for up to 6 months.

Savoy Cabbage Rolls

Servings:20 | Cooking Time: 20 Minutes

Ingredients:
- 1 medium head savoy cabbage
- 3 cups water, divided
- ½ pound ground beef
- 1 cup long-grain rice
- 1 small red bell pepper, seeded and minced
- 1 medium onion, peeled and diced
- 1 cup beef broth
- 1 tablespoon olive oil
- 2 tablespoons minced fresh mint
- 1 teaspoon dried tarragon
- 1 teaspoon salt
- ½ teaspoon ground black pepper
- 2 tablespoons lemon juice

Directions:
1. Wash the cabbage. Remove the large outer leaves and set aside. Remove remaining cabbage leaves and place them in the Instant Pot. Pour in 1 cup water. Lock lid.
2. Press the Steam button and adjust time to 1 minute. Press the Pressure button to change the pressure to Low. When the timer beeps, quick-release the pressure until float valve drops and then unlock lid. Drain the cabbage leaves in a colander and then move them to a cotton towel.
3. In a medium mixing bowl, add the ground beef, rice, bell pepper, onion, broth, olive oil, mint, tarragon, salt, and pepper. Stir to combine.
4. Place the reserved (uncooked) cabbage leaves on the bottom of the Instant Pot.
5. Remove the stem running down the center of each steamed cabbage leaf and tear each leaf in half lengthwise. Place 1 tablespoon of the ground beef mixture in the center of each cabbage piece. Loosely fold the sides of the leaf over the filling and then fold the top and bottom of the leaf over the folded sides. As you complete them, place each stuffed cabbage leaf in the Instant Pot.
6. Pour 2 cups water and the lemon juice over the stuffed cabbage rolls. Lock lid.
7. Press the Manual button and adjust time to 15 minutes. When timer beeps, let pressure release naturally for 10 minutes. Quick-release any additional pressure until float valve drops and then unlock lid.
8. Carefully move the stuffed cabbage rolls to a serving platter. Serve warm.

Pea & Beef Stew

Servings: 6 | Cooking Time: 35 Minutes

Ingredients:
- 1 cup mixed wild mushrooms
- 1 cup green peas
- 1 cup diced potatoes
- 1 lb cubed beef
- 3 sliced carrots
- 1 tsp red pepper flakes
- 2 sliced garlic cloves
- ½ cup dry red wine
- 2 tbsp butter
- 1 diced onion
- 2 cups beef broth
- 14 oz can diced tomatoes

Directions:
1. Melt the butter in your Instant Pot on Sauté. Place the onion and cook for 3 minutes until soft. Add in beef cubes and cook for 5-7 minutes until the meat browns. Add in garlic and cook for 1 minute until fragrant. Pour in red wine and scrape any brown bits from the bottom.
2. Put in potatoes, carrots, red pepper flakes, mushrooms, beef broth, diced tomatoes, and green peas. Seal the lid, select Manual, and cook for 15 minutes on High pressure. When done, perform a quick pressure release and unlock the lid. Serve immediately.

Vegetarian Lentil Soup With Nachos

Servings: 6 | Cooking Time: 40 Minutes

Ingredients:

- 2 ½ cups vegetable broth
- 1 ½ cups tomato sauce
- 1 onion, chopped
- 1 cup dry red lentils
- ½ cup prepared salsa verde
- 2 garlic cloves, minced
- 1 tbsp smoked paprika
- 2 tsp ground cumin
- 1 tsp chili powder
- ¼ tsp cayenne pepper
- Salt and pepper to taste
- Crushed tortilla chips

Directions:

1. Add in tomato sauce, broth, onion, salsa verde, cumin, cayenne pepper, chili powder, garlic, lentils, paprika, salt, and pepper. Seal the lid and cook for 20 minutes on High Pressure. Release pressure naturally for 10 minutes. Garnish with crushed tortilla chips and serve. Enjoy!

Goat Cheese & Beef Steak Salad

Servings: 4 | Cooking Time: 55 Minutes

Ingredients:

- 1 lb rib-eye steak, boneless
- 4 oz fresh arugula
- 1 large tomato, sliced
- ¼ cup fresh goat's cheese
- 4 almonds, chopped
- 4 walnuts, chopped
- 4 hazelnuts
- 3 tbsp olive oil
- 2 cups beef broth
- 2 tbsp red wine vinegar
- 1 tbsp Italian seasoning

Directions:

1. In a bowl, whisk the red wine vinegar, Italian seasoning, and olive oil. Brush each steak with the mixture and place it in your Instant Pot. Pour in the broth and seal the lid. Cook on Meat/Stew for 25 minutes on High. Release the pressure naturally for 10 minutes. Unlock the lid. Remove the steaks along with the broth. Grease the inner pot with oil and hit Sauté. Brown the steaks on both sides for 5-6 minutes. Remove from the pot and chill for 5 minutes before slicing. In a bowl, mix arugula, tomato, cheese, almonds, walnuts, and hazelnuts. Top with steaks and drizzle with red wine mixture. Serve.

Carrot & Broccoli Salad With Hazelnuts

Servings: 4 | Cooking Time: 15 Minutes

Ingredients:

- 1 lb broccoli florets
- 2 carrots, sliced
- 2 green onions, sliced
- 1 tbsp lemon juice
- 1 tsp oregano
- 1 tsp garlic powder
- 2 tbsp hazelnuts, chopped
- 2 tbsp olive oil
- Salt to taste

Directions:

1. Pour 1 cup of water into your Instant Pot and fit in a steamer basket. Place in the broccoli and carrots and seal the lid. Select Manual and cook for 2 minutes.

2. When done, perform a quick pressure release and unlock the lid. Remove the vegetables to iced water for a few minutes. Drain and place in a serving bowl. Add in green onions, lemon juice, oregano, garlic powder, salt, and olive oil and stir to combine. Serve topped with hazelnuts.

Spicy Chicken Chili

Servings:8 | Cooking Time: 40 Minutes

Ingredients:
- 1 tablespoon olive oil
- 1 pound ground chicken
- 1 medium yellow onion, peeled and diced
- 3 cloves garlic, minced
- 3 canned chipotle chilies in adobo sauce
- 1 can dark red kidney beans, drained and rinsed
- 1 can black beans, drained and rinsed
- 1 teaspoon Worcestershire sauce
- 1 can diced tomatoes, including liquid
- 1 can diced green chilies, including liquid
- 1 teaspoon sea salt
- 2 teaspoons hot sauce
- 1 teaspoon smoked paprika
- 1 teaspoon chili powder

Directions:
1. Press the Sauté button on the Instant Pot. Heat oil. Add the ground chicken and onion and stir-fry approximately 5 minutes until chicken is no longer pink.
2. Stir in the remaining ingredients. Lock lid.
3. Press the Meat button and cook for the default time of 35 minutes.
4. When timer beeps, let pressure release naturally until float valve drops and then unlock lid.
5. Ladle into individual bowls and serve warm.

Homemade Chicken & Quinoa Soup

Servings: 6 | Cooking Time: 25 Minutes

Ingredients:
- 2 tbsp canola oil
- 6 spring onions, chopped
- 2 garlic cloves, finely diced
- 1 carrot, chopped
- 2 celery stalks, chopped
- 2 chicken breasts, cubed
- 6 cups chicken broth
- 1 cup quinoa
- Salt and pepper to taste

Directions:
1. Heat canola oil on Sauté. Add in celery, spring onions, garlic, and carrot. Cook for 5 minutes. Add in chicken, quinoa, salt, chicken broth, and pepper. Seal the lid, select Soup/Broth, and cook for 15 minutes on High. Do a quick release. Serve.

Cauliflower & Kale Curry

Servings: 4 | Cooking Time: 10 Minutes

Ingredients:
- 1 lb cauliflower florets
- 1 can coconut milk
- ½ tsp fresh ginger, grated
- 1 lb kale, chopped
- 2 tsp garam masala
- 1 cup tomato sauce
- 1cup vegetable broth
- Salt and pepper to taste

Directions:
1. Mix the cauliflower, coconut milk, kale, garam masala, tomato sauce, ginger, broth, salt, and pepper in your Instant Pot. Seal the lid, select Manual, and cook for 4 minutes on High pressure. When done, perform a quick pressure release and unlock the lid. Serve immediately.

Spicy Egg Casserole With Cheddar Cheese

Servings: 4 | Cooking Time: 35 Minutes

Ingredients:
- ½ lb cheddar, shredded
- 5 eggs, whisked
- 1 onion, sliced
- 1 green chili, chopped
- 1 red bell pepper, chopped
- Salt and pepper to taste
- ¼ tbsp dried basil
- 2 tbsp butter
- ¼ cup parsley, chopped

Directions:
1. Melt butter in your Instant Pot on Sauté. Add in onion and cook for 2-3 minutes until tender. Put in bell pepper and cook for 2 minutes. Transfer to a baking dish. Add in whisked eggs, cheddar cheese, green chilies, basil, salt, and pepper. Pour 1 cup of water into the pot and insert a trivet. Place the dish on the trivet and seal the lid.
2. Select Manual and cook for 10 minutes on High pressure. When done, allow a natural release for 10 minutes and unlock the lid. Garnish with fresh parsley and serve.

Homemade Corn Chowder

Servings:4 | Cooking Time: 30 Minutes

Ingredients:
- 6 slices bacon
- 1 large sweet onion, peeled and diced
- 2 large Yukon Gold potatoes, peeled and diced small
- 6 cups chicken broth
- 1 teaspoon salt
- 1 teaspoon ground black pepper
- 3 cups fresh corn kernels
- 1 tablespoon Italian seasoning
- 1 cup heavy cream

Directions:
1. Line a plate with paper towels.
2. Press the Sauté button on the Instant Pot and fry bacon 2 ½ minutes. Flip bacon and cook for an additional 2 ½ minutes. Remove from pot and set on prepared plate.
3. Add onion and sauté 3–5 minutes until onions are translucent. Add potatoes and continue to sauté 2–3 minutes until potatoes start to brown. Add broth, salt, pepper, corn, and Italian seasoning. Crumble 2 bacon pieces and add to pot. Press the Cancel button. Lock lid.
4. Press the Manual or Pressure Cook button and adjust time to 15 minutes. When timer beeps, quick-release pressure until float valve drops. Unlock lid.
5. Add cream and purée soup in pot with an immersion blender, or use a stand blender and purée in batches.
6. Ladle soup into bowls. Crumble remaining bacon slices and distribute on top of each bowl for garnish. Serve warm.

Chilled Pearl Couscous Salad

Servings:6 | Cooking Time: 10 Minutes

Ingredients:
- 3 tablespoons olive oil, divided
- 1 cup pearl couscous
- 1 cup water
- 1 cup fresh orange juice
- 1 small cucumber, seeded and diced
- 1 small yellow bell pepper, seeded and diced
- 2 small Roma tomatoes, seeded and diced
- ¼ cup slivered almonds
- ¼ cup chopped fresh mint leaves
- 2 tablespoons lemon juice
- 1 teaspoon lemon zest
- ¼ cup feta cheese
- ¼ teaspoon fine sea salt
- 1 teaspoon smoked paprika
- 1 teaspoon garlic powder

Directions:
1. Press the Sauté button on the Instant Pot. Heat 1 tablespoon olive oil, add couscous, and stir-fry for 2–4 minutes until couscous is slightly browned. Add water and orange juice. Lock lid.
2. Press the Manual button and adjust time to 5 minutes. When the timer beeps, let pressure release naturally for 5 minutes. Quick-release any additional pressure until float valve drops and then unlock lid. Drain any liquid.
3. Combine remaining ingredients in a medium bowl. Set aside. Once couscous has cooled, toss it into bowl ingredients. Cover and refrigerate overnight until ready to serve chilled.

Chapter 4 Poultry

Chapter 4 Poultry

Buttermilk Cornish Game Hens

Servings:2 | Cooking Time: 15 Minutes

Ingredients:
- 2 Cornish game hens
- 2 cups buttermilk
- 2 tablespoons Italian seasoning
- 2 teaspoons chili powder
- 1 teaspoon salt
- ½ teaspoon ground black pepper
- 1 medium orange, quartered
- 1 ½ cups water
- 1 tablespoon olive oil

Directions:

1. Pat down Cornish game hens with a paper towel. Set aside.

2. In a large bowl, whisk together buttermilk, Italian seasoning, chili powder, salt, and pepper. Place hens in mixture. Refrigerate covered overnight.

3. Place orange quarters in cavities of hens.

4. Add water to the Instant Pot. Insert steamer basket and place hens in basket. Lock lid.

5. Press the Meat button and adjust time to 10 minutes. When timer beeps, let pressure release naturally for 5 minutes. Quick-release any additional pressure until float valve drops. Unlock lid. Check hens using a meat thermometer to ensure internal temperature is at least 165°F.

6. Transfer hens to a parchment paper–lined baking sheet and brush hens with oil. Remove and discard orange quarters from cavities of hens. Broil 5 minutes.

7. Transfer hens to a serving dish. Serve warm.

Turkey Soup With Noodle

Servings: 6 | Cooking Time: 40 Minutes

Ingredients:
- 1 tbsp olive oil
- 1 onion, minced
- 3 cloves garlic, minced
- 1 turnip, chopped
- 1 cup celery rib, chopped
- 1 tbsp dry basil
- 1 bay leaf
- 6 cups vegetable broth
- 1 lb turkey breasts, cubed
- 8 oz dry egg noodles
- Salt and pepper to taste

Directions:

1. Warm olive oil on Sauté. Stir-fry in garlic and onion for 3 minutes. Mix in celery, bay leaf, basil, and turnip. Pour in 3 cups of broth. Scrape any brown bits from the pan's bottom and add turkey. Seal the lid and cook on High Pressure for 10 minutes. Naturally release the pressure. Transfer turkey breasts to another bowl.

2. Do away with the skin and bones. Using two forks, shred the meat. Set the cooker on Sauté. Transfer the turkey to the pot; add noodles and the remaining broth. Simmer for 10 minutes until noodles are done. Season and serve.

Chimichurri Chicken

Servings: 6 | Cooking Time: 25 Minutes

Ingredients:
- 2 lb chicken breasts
- 1 cup chicken broth
- 1 tsp smoked paprika
- 1 tsp cumin
- Salt and pepper to taste
- 2 cups chimichurri salsa

Directions:
1. Sprinkle chicken breasts with paprika, cumin, salt, and pepper. Place the chicken broth with chicken breasts in your Instant Pot. Seal the lid, select Manual, and cook for 15 minutes on High pressure. Once done, perform a quick pressure release and unlock the lid. Cut the chicken into slices and top with chimichurri sauce. Serve.

Okra & Rice Chicken With Spring Onions

Servings: 4 | Cooking Time: 30 Minutes

Ingredients:
- 6 garlic cloves, grated
- ¼ cup tomato puree
- ½ cup soy sauce
- 2 tbsp rice vinegar
- 2 tbsp olive oil
- 4 chicken breasts, chopped
- 1 cup rice, rinsed
- ½ tsp salt
- 2 cups frozen okra
- 1 tbsp cornstarch
- 2 tsp toasted sesame seeds
- 4 spring onions, chopped

Directions:
1. In your Instant Pot, mix garlic, tomato puree, vinegar, soy sauce, ½ cup of water, and oil. Add in the chicken and toss it to coat. In an ovenproof bowl, mix 2 cups of water, salt, and rice. Set a steamer rack on top of the chicken. Lower the bowl onto the rack. Seal the lid.
2. Cook on High Pressure for 10 minutes. Release the pressure quickly. Stir in okra. Allow the okra steam in the residual heat for 3 minutes. Take the trivet and bowl from the pot. Set the chicken on a plate. Press Sauté.

3. In a bowl, mix 1 tbsp water and cornstarch until smooth. Stir into the sauce and cook for 3-4 minutes until thickened. Divide the rice, chicken, and okra between 4 bowls. Drizzle with sauce, garnish with spring onions and sesame seeds, and serve.

Chicken & Quinoa Soup

Servings: 6 | Cooking Time: 30 Minutes

Ingredients:
- 2 tbsp butter
- 1 cup red onion, chopped
- 1 cup carrots, chopped
- 1 cup celery, chopped
- 2 chicken breasts, cubed
- 4 cups chicken broth
- 6 oz quinoa, rinsed
- 2 tbsp parsley, chopped
- Salt and pepper to taste
- 4 oz mascarpone cheese
- 1 cup milk
- 1 cup heavy cream

Directions:
1. Melt butter on Sauté in your Instant Pot. Add carrots, onion, and celery and cook for 5 minutes. Add in broth, parsley, quinoa, and chicken. Season with pepper and salt. Seal the lid. Cook on High Pressure for 10 minutes. Release the pressure quickly. Add mascarpone to the soup and stir to melt it completely. Stir in heavy cream and milk until the soup is thickened and creamy.

Creamy Mascarpone Chicken

Servings: 4 | Cooking Time: 30 Minutes

Ingredients:
- 8 bacon slices, cooked and crumbled
- 1 lb chicken breasts
- 8 oz mascarpone cheese
- 1 tbsp Dijon mustard
- 1 tsp ranch seasoning
- 3 tbsp cornstarch
- ½ cup cheddar, shredded

Directions:
1. Place the chicken breasts, mustard, and mascarpone cheese in your Instant Pot. Add in ranch seasoning and 1 cup of water. Seal the lid, select Manual, and cook for 15 minutes on High pressure. Once ready, perform

a quick pressure release and unlock the lid. Remove the chicken and shred it. Add in cornstarch, shredded chicken, cheese, and bacon and cook for 3 minutes on Sauté. Lock the lid and let chill for a few minutes. Serve.

Chicken And Gnocchi Alfredo With Vegetables

Servings:6 | Cooking Time: 3 Minutes

Ingredients:
- 1 package gnocchi
- 1 jar Alfredo sauce
- ½ cup chicken broth
- 1 cup chopped cooked chicken
- 1 can mushroom stems and pieces, drained
- 1 can sweet peas and carrots, drained

Directions:
1. In the Instant Pot, add gnocchi and sauce. Pour broth into empty sauce jar, close lid of jar, and shake. Pour mixture into pot. Stir in remaining ingredients. Lock lid.
2. Press the Manual or Pressure Cook button and adjust time to 3 minutes. When timer beeps, let pressure release naturally for 5 minutes. Quick-release any additional pressure until float valve drops. Unlock lid.
3. Transfer to bowls. Serve warm.

Chicken Breast Parmesan With Mushrooms

Servings:8 | Cooking Time: 20 Minutes

Ingredients:
- ½ cup all-purpose flour
- ½ teaspoon salt
- ½ teaspoon ground black pepper
- 2 pounds boneless, skinless chicken breast, cut in 1" cubes
- 2 tablespoons olive oil
- 1 large onion, peeled and diced
- 1 tablespoon Italian seasoning
- 2 tablespoons tomato paste
- ½ cup chicken broth
- 1 can tomato sauce
- 1 teaspoon balsamic vinegar
- 2 cups sliced white mushrooms
- 2 teaspoons honey
- 2 tablespoons chopped fresh parsley

- 1 cup grated Parmesan cheese

Directions:
1. Add the flour, salt, and pepper to a large zip-closure bag; seal and shake to mix. Add chicken cubes to the bag, seal, and shake to coat the meat in the flour.
2. Press the Sauté button on the Instant Pot. Heat the oil and add the chicken and onion. Stir-fry for 3–5 minutes until onions are translucent. Stir in Italian seasoning and tomato paste. Sauté for 2 minutes. Stir in the broth, tomato sauce, vinegar, mushrooms, and honey. Lock lid.
3. Press the Manual button and adjust time to 12 minutes. When timer beeps, let pressure release naturally for 10 minutes. Quick-release any additional pressure until float valve drops and then unlock lid. Check the chicken using a meat thermometer to ensure the internal temperature is at least 165°F.
4. Stir the cooked chicken and sauce in the Instant Pot. Transfer to a serving dish. Garnish with parsley and grated Parmesan cheese and serve warm.

Savory Orange Chicken

Servings: 6 | Cooking Time: 25 Minutes

Ingredients:
- 2 tbsp olive oil
- 6 chicken breasts, cubed
- 1/3 cup chicken stock
- ¼ cup soy sauce
- 2 tbsp brown sugar
- 1 tbsp lemon juice
- 1 tbsp garlic powder
- 1 tsp chili sauce
- 1 cup orange juice
- Salt and pepper to taste
- 1 tbsp cornstarch

Directions:
1. Warm oil on Sauté in your Instant Pot. Sear the chicken for 5 minutes until browned, stirring occasionally. Set aside in a bowl. In the pot, mix orange juice, chicken stock, sugar, chili sauce, garlic powder, lemon juice, and soy sauce. Stir in chicken to coat. Seal the lid.
2. Cook on High Pressure for 7 minutes. Release the pressure quickly. Take ¼ cup liquid from the pot to a bowl and stir in cornstarch to dissolve. Pour the sauce in the pot and stir until the color is consistent. Press Sauté and cook the sauce for 2-3 minutes until thickened. Season with pepper and salt. Serve warm.

Thai Chicken Thighs

Servings:5 | Cooking Time: 15 Minutes

Ingredients:
- 3 pounds chicken legs
- 1 teaspoon fine sea salt
- ½ cup canned coconut milk
- ½ cup chicken broth
- 2 tablespoons coconut aminos
- 1 tablespoon tomato paste
- 1 tablespoon honey
- 1 teaspoon lime zest
- 1 tablespoon fresh lime juice
- 1 tablespoon sriracha
- 3 cloves garlic, minced
- ½» knob of gingerroot, peeled and grated
- ¼ cup chopped fresh cilantro

Directions:
1. Pat chicken legs dry with a paper towel. On a plate, season chicken with salt. Place in the Instant Pot.
2. In a medium bowl, whisk together remaining ingredients. Pour mixture over chicken. Lock lid.
3. Press the Poultry button and cook for the default time of 15 minutes. When timer beeps, let pressure release naturally for 10 minutes. Quick-release any additional pressure until float valve drops and then unlock lid. Check the chicken using a meat thermometer to ensure the internal temperature is at least 165°F.
4. Remove chicken from pot, transfer to a platter, and serve warm.

Buttered Chicken With Artichokes

Servings: 4 | Cooking Time: 35 Minutes

Ingredients:
- 1 lb chicken breasts, chopped
- 2 artichokes, trimmed, halved
- 3 tbsp butter, melted
- 1 lemon, juiced
- Salt and pepper to taste
- 1 tbsp rosemary, chopped

Directions:
1. Heat 1 tbsp butter on Sauté in your Instant Pot and cook the chicken for a minute per side until slightly golden. Pour in 1 cup of water, seal the lid, and cook on High Pressure for 13 minutes. Do a quick release. Set aside.
2. Insert a trivet in the pot. Rub the artichoke halves with half of the lemon juice and arrange on the trivet. Seal the lid and cook on Steam for 3 minutes. Do a quick release. Combine artichoke and chicken in a large bowl. Stir in salt, pepper, and lemon juice. Drizzle the remaining butter over and sprinkle with rosemary to serve.

Tasty Chicken Breasts With Bbq Sauce

Servings: 6 | Cooking Time: 20 Minutes

Ingredients:
- 2 lb chicken breasts
- 1 tsp salt
- 1 ½ cups barbecue sauce
- 1 small onion, minced
- 1 cup carrots, chopped
- 4 garlic cloves

Directions:
1. Rub salt onto the chicken and place it in the Instant Pot. Add onion, carrots, garlic, and barbeque sauce; toss to coat. Seal the lid, press Manual, and cook on High for 15 minutes. Do a quick release. Shred the chicken and stir into the sauce. Serve.

Pancetta & Cabbage Chicken Thighs

Servings: 4 | Cooking Time: 30 Minutes

Ingredients:
- 4 chicken thighs, boneless skinless
- 1 tbsp lard
- 4 slices pancetta, diced
- Salt and pepper to taste
- 1 cup chicken broth
- 1 tbsp Dijon mustard
- 1 lb green cabbage, shredded
- 2 tbsp parsley, chopped

Directions:
1. Melt lard on Sauté in your Instant Pot. Fry pancetta for 5 minutes until crisp. Set aside. Season chicken with pepper and salt. Sear in the cooker for 2 minutes on each side until browned. In a bowl, mix mustard and broth.
2. In the cooker, add pancetta, and chicken broth mixture. Seal the lid and cook on High Pressure for 6 minutes. Release the pressure quickly. Open the lid, mix in green cabbage, seal again, and cook again on High Pressure for 2 minutes. Release the pressure quickly. Serve with sprinkled parsley.

Spring Onion Buffalo Wings

Servings: 6 | Cooking Time: 30 Minutes

Ingredients:
- 2 lb chicken wings, sectioned
- 2 spring onions, sliced diagonally
- ½ cup hot pepper sauce
- 1 tbsp Worcestershire sauce
- 3 tbsp butter
- Sea salt to taste
- 2 tbsp sugar, light brown

Directions:
1. Combine hot sauce, Worcestershire sauce, butter, salt, and brown sugar in a bowl and microwave for 20 seconds until the butter melts. Pour 1 cup of water into your Instant Pot and fit in a trivet. Place the chicken wings on the trivet and seal the lid. Select Manual and cook for 10 minutes on High pressure.
2. Once done, perform a quick pressure release and unlock the lid. Remove chicken wings to a baking dish and brush the top with marinade. Broil for 4-5 minutes, turn the wings and brush more marinade. Broil for 4-5 minutes more. Top with spring onions and serve.

Hot Chicken With Garlic & Mushrooms

Servings: 4 | Cooking Time: 30 Minutes

Ingredients:
- 1 cup button mushrooms, chopped
- 1 lb chicken breasts, cubed
- 2 cups chicken broth
- 2 tbsp flour
- 1 tsp cayenne pepper
- Salt and pepper to taste
- 2 tbsp olive oil
- 2 garlic cloves, chopped

Directions:
1. Warm the olive oil in your Instant Pot on Sauté. Add mushrooms, garlic, and chicken, season with salt, and stir-fry for 5 minutes, stirring occasionally until the veggies are tender. Pour in the chicken broth. Seal the lid. Cook on High Pressure for 8 minutes. Release the steam naturally for 10 minutes and stir in flour, cayenne, and black pepper. Cook for 5 minutes on Sauté. Serve warm.

Mediterranean Duck With Olives

Servings: 4 | Cooking Time: 20 Minutes

Ingredients:
- ½ cup sun-dried tomatoes, chopped
- 1 lb duck breasts, halved
- 2 tbsp olive oil
- ½ tbsp Italian seasoning
- Salt and pepper to taste
- 2 garlic cloves, minced
- ½ cup chicken stock
- ¾ cup heavy cream
- 1 cup kale, chopped
- ½ cup Parmesan, grated
- 10 Kalamata olives, pitted

Directions:
1. Combine olive oil, Italian seasoning, pepper, salt, and garlic in a bowl. Add in the duck breasts and toss to coat. Set your Instant Pot to Sauté. Place in duck breasts and cook for 5-6 minutes on both sides. Pour in chicken stock and seal the lid. Select Manual and cook for 4 minutes.
2. When done, perform a quick pressure release and unlock the lid. Mix in heavy cream, tomatoes, Kalamata olives, and kale and cook for 5 minutes on Sauté. Serve topped with Parmesan cheese.

Fabulous Orange Chicken Stew

Servings: 4 | Cooking Time: 55 Minutes

Ingredients:
- 1 cup fire-roasted tomatoes, diced
- 1 lb chicken breasts
- 1 tbsp chili powder
- Salt and pepper to taste
- 1 cup orange juice
- 2 cups chicken broth

Directions:
1. Season the chicken with chili powder, salt, and pepper, and place in your Instant Pot. Add fire-roasted tomatoes and cook on Sauté for 10 minutes, stirring occasionally. Pour in the broth and orange juice. Seal the lid and cook on Poultry for 25 minutes on High. Release the pressure naturally for 10 minutes. Serve immediately.

Chicken With Chili & Lime

Servings: 4 | Cooking Time: 25 Minutes

Ingredients:
- 1 lb chicken breasts
- ¾ cup chicken broth
- Juice and zest of 1 lime
- 1 red chili, chopped
- 1 tsp cumin
- 1 tsp onion powder
- 2 garlic cloves, minced
- 1 tsp mustard powder
- 1 bay leaf
- Salt and pepper to taste

Directions:

1. Place the chicken breasts, chicken broth, lime juice, lime zest, red chili, cumin, onion powder, garlic cloves, mustard powder, bay leaf, salt, and pepper in your Instant Pot. Seal the lid, select Manual, and cook for 10 minutes on High. When ready, allow a natural release. Remove chicken and shred it. Discard the bay leaf. Top the chicken with cooking juices and serve.

Tuscan Vegetable Chicken Stew

Servings: 4 | Cooking Time: 60 Minutes

Ingredients:
- 14 oz broccoli and cauliflower florets
- A handful of yellow wax beans, whole
- 1 whole chicken
- 1 onion, peeled, chopped
- 1 potato, peeled, chopped
- 3 carrots, chopped
- 1 tomato, peeled, chopped
- ¼ cup extra virgin olive oil
- Salt and pepper to taste

Directions:

1. Warm 3 tbsp olive oil in your Instant Pot on Sauté. Stir-fry the onion for 3-4 minutes on Sauté. Add the carrots and sauté for 5 more minutes. Add the remaining oil, broccoli, potato, wax beans, tomato, salt, and pepper and top with chicken. Add 1 cup of water and seal the lid. Cook on High Pressure for 30 minutes. Release the pressure naturally for about 10 minutes. Carefully unlock the lid. Serve warm.

Cheesy Chicken Chile Verde

Servings:4 | Cooking Time: 13 Minutes

Ingredients:
- 1 pound boneless, skinless chicken breasts, cut in 1" cubes
- 1 teaspoon salt
- ½ teaspoon ground black pepper
- 2 cups water
- 2 cans diced green chiles
- ½ cup shredded Colby jack cheese
- 4 cups cooked rice

Directions:

1. Season chicken with salt and pepper.
2. Preheat oven to broiler at 500°F.
3. Add water to the Instant Pot and insert steam rack. Add chicken and green chiles to baking dish and place on steam rack. Lock lid.
4. Press the Manual or Pressure Cook button and adjust time to 10 minutes. When timer beeps, let pressure release naturally for 10 minutes. Quick-release any additional pressure until float valve drops. Unlock lid. Check chicken using a meat thermometer to ensure internal temperature is at least 165°F.
5. Line a baking sheet with parchment paper. Transfer chicken to prepared baking sheet. Sprinkle cheese evenly over chicken.
6. Place sheet under a broiler 3 minutes.
7. Serve warm over rice.

Brussels Sprouts & Zucchini Chicken

Servings: 4 | Cooking Time: 30 Minutes

Ingredients:
- 4 chicken thighs, boneless and skinless
- 1 cup chicken stock
- ½ cauliflower head, chopped
- 2 tomatoes, chopped
- ½ lb Brussels sprouts
- 2 zucchinis, chopped
- 1 onion, chopped
- 3 tbsp olive oil
- 1 tsp salt

Directions:
1. Heat the olive oil in your Instant Pot on Sauté. Stir-fry onion, cauliflower, tomatoes, sprouts, and zucchinis for 5 minutes until tender. Add in the chicken stock, chicken thighs, and salt and seal the lid. Cook on manual for 15 minutes on High. Do a quick release. Serve warm.

North African Turkey Stew

Servings: 4 | Cooking Time: 60 Minutes

Ingredients:
- 1 lb turkey breast, cubed
- 2 tbsp butter
- 1 onion, diced
- ½ tsp garlic powder
- 2 tsp ras el hanout
- 1 carrot, sliced
- 2 celery stalks, chopped
- 15.5 oz chickpeas, drained
- 2 oz green olives, pitted
- 3 ½ cups chicken broth
- Salt and pepper to taste
- 2 tbsp cilantro, chopped

Directions:
1. Melt butter in your Instant Pot on Sauté and cook the onion, carrot, and celery for 3-4 minutes. Stir in turkey breast and cook until browned, about 4-5 minutes. Mix in garlic powder, ras el hanout, salt, pepper, chickpeas, and chicken broth. Seal the lid, select Manual, and cook for 25 minutes on High pressure. When done, allow a natural release for 10 minutes and unlock the lid. Serve topped with green olives and cilantro.

Filipino-style Chicken Congee

Servings: 6 | Cooking Time: 55 Minutes

Ingredients:
- 6 chicken drumsticks
- 1 cup Jasmine rice
- 1 tbsp fresh ginger, grated
- 1 tbsp fish sauce
- 4 green onions, chopped
- 3 hard-boiled eggs, halved

Directions:
1. Place chicken, rice, 6 cups of water, fish sauce, and ginger in your Instant Pot and stir. Seal the lid, select Manual, and cook for 25 minutes on High pressure.
2. When done, allow a natural release for 10 minutes. Remove the chicken and shred it. Put shredded chicken back in the pot and cook for 10 minutes on Sauté. Top with eggs and green onions and serve.

Sticky Chicken Wings

Servings: 6 | Cooking Time: 35 Minutes + Marinating Time

Ingredients:
- 2 lb chicken wings
- 3 tbsp light brown sugar
- 2 tbsp soy sauce
- 1 small lime, juiced
- ½ tsp sea salt
- 1 tsp five-spice powder

Directions:
1. Combine soy sauce, lime juice, five-spice powder, brown sugar, and salt in a bowl. Place chicken wing and marinade in a resealable bag and shake it. Transfer to the fridge and let marinate for 30 minutes.
2. Pour 1/2 cup of water and marinate chicken wings with the juices in your Instant Pot. Seal the lid, select Manual, and cook for 15 minutes on High pressure. When done, allow a natural release for 10 minutes and unlock the lid. Cook on Sauté until the sauce thickens. Serve.

Bell Pepper & Chicken Stew

Servings: 4 | Cooking Time: 30 Minutes

Ingredients:
- 1 lb chicken breasts, cubed
- 2 potatoes, peeled, chopped
- 5 bell peppers, chopped
- 2 carrots, chopped
- 2 ½ cups chicken broth
- 1 tomato, roughly chopped
- 2 tbsp chopped parsley
- 3 tbsp extra virgin olive oil
- 1 tsp cayenne pepper

Directions:
1. Warm the olive oil on Sauté in your Instant Pot. Stir-fry the bell peppers and carrots for 3 minutes. Add in the potatoes and tomato. Sprinkle with cayenne and stir well. Top with the chicken, pour in the broth, and seal the lid. Cook on High Pressure for 13 minutes. When ready, do a quick pressure release. Sprinkle with parsley and serve.

Za'atar Chicken With Baby Potatoes

Servings: 4 | Cooking Time: 30 Minutes

Ingredients:
- 1 lb chicken thighs
- ½ lb baby potatoes, halved
- 2 tbsp olive oil
- 1 tbsp za'atar seasoning
- 1 garlic clove, minced
- 1 large onion, sliced
- Salt and pepper to taste

Directions:
1. Warm the olive oil in your Instant Pot on Sauté. Place in onion and garlic and cook for 2 minutes. Add in chicken thighs and cook for 4-6 minutes on both sides. Scatter with za´atar seasoning, salt, pepper, potatoes, and pour in 1 cup of water. Seal the lid, select Manual, and cook for 15 minutes on High pressure.
2. Once ready, perform a quick pressure release and unlock the lid. Remove the chicken and shred it. Put chicken back to the pot and toss to coat. Serve right away.

Chicken & Pepper Cacciatore

Servings: 4 | Cooking Time: 50 Minutes

Ingredients:
- 4 chicken thighs, with the bone, skin removed
- 3 mixed bell peppers, cut into strips
- 2 tbsp olive oil
- Salt and pepper to taste
- 2 garlic cloves, minced
- 1 diced onion
- 1 cup canned diced tomatoes
- 2 tbsp chopped rosemary
- ½ tsp oregano
- 10 black olives, pitted

Directions:
1. Warm olive oil in your Instant Pot on Sauté. Sprinkle chicken with salt and pepper and cook in the pot for 2-3 minutes per side; reserve. Add bell pepper, garlic, and onion to the pot and cook for 5 minutes. Stir in tomatoes, oregano, and 1 cup water and return the chicken. Seal the lid, select Manual, and cook for 20 minutes on High pressure. When done, allow a natural release for 10 minutes and unlock the lid. Serve topped with black olives and rosemary.

Thai Chicken

Servings: 4 | Cooking Time: 25 Minutes

Ingredients:
- 1 lb chicken thighs
- 1 cup lime juice
- 4 tbsp red curry paste
- ½ cup fish sauce
- 2 tbsp brown sugar
- 1 red chili pepper, sliced
- 2 tbsp olive oil
- 1 tsp ginger, grated
- 2 tbsp cilantro, chopped

Directions:
1. Combine lime juice, red curry paste, fish sauce, olive oil, brown sugar, ginger, and cilantro in a bowl. Add in chicken thighs and toss to coat. Transfer to your Instant Pot and pour in 1 cup water.
2. Seal the lid, select Manual, and cook for 15 minutes on High. When done, perform a quick pressure release. Top with red chili slices and serve.

Black Bean And Corn Salsa Chicken Breasts

Servings:4 | Cooking Time: 15 Minutes

Ingredients:
- 2 pounds boneless, skinless chicken breasts
- 1 jar black bean and corn salsa
- ½ cup chicken broth

Directions:
1. Place all ingredients in the Instant Pot. Lock lid.
2. Press the Manual or Pressure Cook button and adjust time to 15 minutes. When timer beeps, let pressure release naturally for 10 minutes. Quick-release any additional pressure until float valve drops. Unlock lid. Check chicken using a meat thermometer to ensure internal temperature is at least 165°F.
3. Transfer chicken and salsa to a serving dish. Serve warm.

Chicken With Honey-lime Sauce

Servings: 4 | Cooking Time: 30 Minutes

Ingredients:
- 4 chicken breasts, cut into chunks
- 1 onion, diced
- 4 garlic cloves, smashed
- 1 tbsp honey
- 3 tbsp soy sauce
- 2 tbsp lime juice
- 2 tsp sesame oil
- 1 tsp rice vinegar
- 1 tbsp cornstarch
- Salt and pepper to taste

Directions:
1. Mix garlic, onion, and chicken in your Instant Pot. In a bowl, combine honey, sesame oil, lime juice, soy sauce, and rice vinegar. Pour over the chicken mixture. Seal the lid and cook on High Pressure for 15 minutes. Release the pressure quickly. Mix 1 tbsp water and cornstarch until well dissolved; Stir into the sauce, add salt and pepper to taste. Press Sauté. Simmer the sauce and cook for 2 to 3 minutes as you stir until thickened.

Chapter 5 Pork, Beef & Lamb

Cherry-rosemary Pork Tenderloin

Servings:6 | Cooking Time: 30 Minutes

Ingredients:
- 2 tablespoons avocado oil
- 2 pork tenderloins, halved
- ½ cup balsamic vinegar
- ¼ cup olive oil
- ¼ cup cherry preserves
- ½ teaspoon sea salt
- ¼ teaspoon ground black pepper
- ¼ cup finely chopped fresh rosemary
- 4 garlic cloves, minced

Directions:
1. Press the Sauté button on the Instant Pot. Heat oil. Brown pork on all sides, about 2 minutes per side.
2. In a small bowl, whisk remaining ingredients together and pour over the pork. Lock lid.
3. Press the Manual button and adjust time to 20 minutes. When timer beeps, let the pressure release naturally for 5 minutes. Quick-release any additional pressure until float valve drops and then unlock lid.
4. Transfer tenderloin to a cutting board. Let rest for 5 minutes. Slice into medallions and serve.

Mushroom & Pork Stroganoff

Servings: 4 | Cooking Time: 35 Minutes

Ingredients:
- 1 cup button mushrooms, sliced
- 1 lb pork loin, cut into strips
- 2 tbsp olive oil
- 1 leek, chopped
- 1 celery stalk, chopped
- 2 cups vegetable broth
- 2 tsp Dijon mustard
- ½ cup sour cream
- ½ cup white wine
- Salt and pepper to taste
- 2 tbsp parsley, chopped

Directions:
1. Warm the oil in your Instant Pot on Sauté. Sprinkle pork loin with salt and pepper, place it in the pot and brown on all sides. Set aside. Add leek, mushrooms, and celery to the pot and cook for 3 minutes. Pour in wine and scrape any brown bits from the bottom. Stir in vegetable broth and Dijon mustard. Put pork loin back to the pot.
2. Seal the lid. Select Manual and cook for 12 minutes on High. Once ready, allow a natural release for 10 minutes and unlock the lid. Mix in sour cream and simmer for 1 minute on Sauté. Top with parsley and serve.

T-bone Steaks With Basil & Mustard

Servings: 4 | Cooking Time: 40 Minutes + Marinating Time

Ingredients:
- 1 lb T-bone steak
- Salt and pepper to taste
- 2 tbsp Dijon mustard
- ¼ cup oil
- ½ tsp dried basil, crushed

Directions:
1. Whisk together oil, mustard, salt, pepper, and basil. Brush each steak and Refrigerate for 1 hour. Then, insert a steamer tray in the Instant Pot. Pour in 1 cup of water and arrange the steaks on the tray. Seal the lid and cook on Manual for 25 minutes on High. Do a quick release. Discard the liquid, remove the tray, and hit Sauté. Brown the steaks for 5 minutes, turning once.

German Pork With Sauerkraut

Servings: 4 | Cooking Time: 40 Minutes

Ingredients:
- 2 lb pork belly, cut into 2-inch pieces
- 3 tbsp lard
- 2 garlic cloves, minced
- 1 onion, chopped
- 1 cup chicken broth
- 5 cups sauerkraut
- 1 tsp paprika
- 1 cup canned diced tomatoes
- 1 tsp cumin
- 2 tbsp parsley, chopped
- Salt and pepper to taste

Directions:
1. Sprinkle the pork with salt and pepper. Melt lard in your Instant Pot on Sauté. Place the pork, onion, and garlic and cook for 5-6 minutes. Stir in paprika and cumin. Put in sauerkraut, chicken broth, tomatoes, and 1/2 cup of water and seal the lid. Select Manual and cook for 30 minutes on High pressure. Once over, perform a quick pressure release and unlock the lid. Serve with parsley.

Traditional French Beef Stew

Servings: 5 | Cooking Time: 55 Minutes

Ingredients:
- 1 lb boneless chuck steak, cut into chunks
- 2 cups portobello mushrooms, quartered
- ¼ cup flour
- Salt and pepper to taste
- 1 cup pancetta, chopped
- ½ cup red burgundy wine
- 1 ¼ cups beef broth
- 1 carrot, diced
- 4 shallots, chopped
- 3 garlic cloves, crushed
- 2 tbsp parsley, chopped

Directions:
1. Toss beef with black pepper, salt, and flour in a large bowl to coat. Set the Instant Pot to Sauté. Cook pancetta for 5 minutes until brown and crispy. Pour in approximately half the beef and cook for 5 minutes on each side until browned all over. Transfer the pancetta and beef to a plate. Sear remaining beef and transfer to the plate.

2. Add beef broth and wine to the cooker to deglaze the pan, scrape the pan's bottom to get rid of any browned bits of food. Return beef and pancetta to cooker and stir in garlic, carrot, shallots, and mushrooms. Seal the lid and cook on High Pressure for 32 minutes. Release the pressure quickly. Garnish with parsley and serve.

Moroccan Beef & Cherry Stew

Servings: 4 | Cooking Time: 1 Hour 20 Minutes

Ingredients:
- 1 ½ lb stewing beef, trimmed
- ¼ cup toasted almonds, slivered
- 2 tbsp olive oil
- 1 onion, chopped
- 1 tsp ground cinnamon
- ½ tsp paprika
- ½ tsp turmeric
- ½ tsp salt
- ¼ tsp ground ginger
- ¼ tsp ground allspice
- 1-star anise
- 1 cup water
- 1 tbsp honey
- 1 cup dried cherries, halved

Directions:
1. Set the Instant Pot to Sauté and warm olive oil. Add in onion and cook for 3 minutes. Mix in beef and cook for 2 minutes each side until browned. Stir in anise, cinnamon, turmeric, allspice, salt, paprika, and ginger; cook for 2 minutes until aromatic. Add in honey and water. Seal the lid, press Meat/Stew, and cook on High for 50 minutes.

2. In a bowl, soak dried cherries in hot water until softened. Once ready, release pressure naturally for 15 minutes. Drain cherries and stir into the tagine. Top with toasted almonds before serving.

Boeuf Bourguignon

Servings: 4 | Cooking Time: 63 Minutes

Ingredients:
- 1 lb flank steak
- 2 tbsp olive oil
- 1 cup pearl onions
- 2 garlic cloves, minced
- 1 cups crimini mushrooms
- 1 carrot, sliced
- 4 oz bacon, chopped
- 1 cup beef broth
- 1 cup Burgundy red wine
- Salt and pepper to taste
- 1 bay leaf
- 2 tbsp thyme, chopped

Directions:
1. Warm the oil in your Instant Pot on Sauté. Place in the steak and cook for 6-8 minutes in total. Set aside. Add onions, garlic, mushrooms, carrots, and bacon to the pot and cook for 4-5 minutes. Stir in beef broth and wine.

2. Put the meat back to the pot and salt, pepper, and bay leaf and seal the lid. Select Manual and cook for 30 minutes on High. When over, allow a natural release for 10 minutes, then perform a quick pressure release, and unlock the lid. Discard bay leaf. Top with thyme.

Tasty Cajun Pork Chops

Servings: 4 | Cooking Time: 80 Minutes

Ingredients:
- 2 lb pork chops
- 1 cup beef broth
- 1 onion, diced
- 2 tbsp potato starch
- 1 carrot, chopped
- Marinade
- 2 tbsp fish sauce
- ½ tsp Cajun seasoning
- 2 tsp garlic, minced
- ½ cup soy sauce
- 1 tbsp sesame oil

Directions:
1. Combine fish sauce, Cajun seasoning, garlic, soy sauce, and sesame oil in a bowl. Add in the pork chops and let marinate for 30 minutes. Coat the pressure cooker with cooking spray. Add onion and carrot and cook until soft on Sauté. Add the pork chops along with the marinade. Whisk in the broth and starch. Seal the lid and cook for 40 minutes on Meat/Stew. Do a quick release and serve.

Chickpea & Pork Stew With Bell Peppers

Servings: 6 | Cooking Time: 30 Minutes

Ingredients:
- 2 lb boneless pork shoulder, cubed
- 2 tbsp olive oil
- 1 white onion, chopped
- 15 oz canned chickpeas
- ½ cup sweet paprika
- 2 tsp salt
- 1 tbsp chili powder
- 1 bay leaf
- 2 red bell peppers, diced
- 6 cloves garlic, minced
- 1 tbsp cornstarch

Directions:
1. Set to Sauté, add pork and oil, and allow cooking for 5 minutes until browned. Add in the onion, paprika, bay leaf, salt, 1 ½ cups of water, chickpeas, and chili powder. Seal the lid and cook on High Pressure for 8 minutes.

2. Do a quick release and discard bay leaf. Remove 1 cup of cooking liquid from the pot; add to a blender alongside garlic, water, cornstarch, and red bell peppers, and blend well until smooth. Add the blended mixture into the stew and mix well. Plate and serve immediately.

Red Wine Beef & Vegetable Hotpot

Servings: 6 | Cooking Time: 40 Minutes

Ingredients:
- 2 sweet potatoes, cut into chunks
- 2 lb stewing beef meat
- ¾ cup red wine
- 1 tbsp ghee
- 6 oz tomato paste
- 6 oz baby carrots, chopped
- 1 onion, finely chopped
- ½ tsp salt
- 4 cups beef broth

- ½ cup green peas
- 1 tsp dried thyme
- 3 garlic cloves, crushed

Directions:

1. Heat ghee on Sauté. Add beef and brown for 5-6 minutes. Add onion and garlic, and keep stirring for 3 more minutes. Add the sweet potatoes, wine, tomato paste, carrots, salt, broth, green peas, and thyme and seal the lid. Cook on Meat/Stew for 20 minutes on High Pressure. Do a quick release. Serve.

Swiss Steak And Potatoes

Servings:6 | Cooking Time: 35 Minutes

Ingredients:

- 2½ pounds beef round steak
- 1 teaspoon sea salt
- ½ teaspoon ground black pepper
- 2 tablespoons olive oil, divided
- 1 medium yellow onion, peeled and diced
- 2 stalks celery, diced
- 1 large green bell pepper, seeded and diced
- 1 cup tomato juice
- 1 cup beef broth
- 6 large carrots, peeled and cut into 1" pieces
- 6 medium Yukon gold potatoes, diced large
- 4 teaspoons butter

Directions:

1. Cut the round steak into 6 serving-sized pieces and season both sides with salt and pepper.
2. Press the Sauté button on the Instant Pot. Heat 1 tablespoon oil. Add 3 pieces of meat and sear for 3 minutes on each side. Move to a platter and repeat with the remaining 1 tablespoon oil and the other 3 pieces of meat.
3. Leave the last 3 pieces of browned meat in the Instant Pot; add the onion, celery, and green pepper on top of them. Lay in the other 3 pieces of meat and pour the tomato juice and broth over them. Place the carrots and potatoes on top of the meat. Lock lid.
4. Press the Manual button and adjust time to 20 minutes. When timer beeps, quick-release pressure until float valve drops and then unlock lid.
5. Transfer the potatoes, carrots, and meat to a serving platter. Cover and keep warm.
6. Skim any fat from the juices remaining in the Instant Pot. Press the Sauté button on the Instant Pot, press Adjust button and change temperature to Less, and simmer the juices unlidded for 5 minutes.

7. Whisk in the butter 1 teaspoon at a time. Serve the resulting gravy available at the table to pour over the meat. Serve immediately.

Oregano Pork With Pears & Dijon Mustard

Servings: 6 | Cooking Time: 60 Minutes

Ingredients:

- 3 lb pork roast
- 2 pears, peeled and sliced
- 3 tbsp Dijon mustard
- 1 tbsp dried oregano
- ½ cup white wine
- 1 tbsp garlic, minced
- 1 tbsp olive oil
- Salt and pepper to taste

Directions:

1. Brush the pork with mustard. Heat oil on Sauté and sear the pork on all sides for 6minutes. Stir in pears, oregano, wine, 1 cup of water, garlic, salt, and pepper. Seal the lid and cook for 40 minutes on Meat/Stew on High Pressure. Release the pressure naturally for 10 minutes.

Beef Steak With Mustard Sauce

Servings: 4 | Cooking Time: 55 Minutes

Ingredients:

- 1 lb flank steak, sliced
- 2 tbsp olive oil
- Salt and pepper to taste
- ½ cup beef broth
- ¼ cup apple cider vinegar
- 1 tbsp onion powder
- 1 tbsp Worcestershire sauce
- 1 cup heavy cream
- 1 tbsp yellow mustard

Directions:

1. Warm 1 tbsp of olive oil in your Instant Pot on Sauté. Season the flank steak with onion powder, salt, and pepper and place in the pot; brown for 4-5 minutes on both sides. Stir in beef broth, vinegar, and Worcestershire sauce and seal the lid. Cook on Meat/Stew for 30 minutes.
2. Once ready, allow a natural release for 10 minutes, then perform a quick pressure release, and unlock the lid. Mix in heavy cream and mustard. Serve immedi-

ately.

3. Seal the lid, select Manual, and cook for 35 minutes on High pressure. Once done, allow a natural release for 10 minutes, then perform a quick pressure release, and unlock the lid. Serve with vegetables or potatoes.

Garlic-spicy Ground Pork With Peas

Servings: 6 | Cooking Time: 55 Minutes

Ingredients:
- 2 lb ground pork
- 1 onion, diced
- 1 can diced tomatoes
- 1 can peas
- 5 garlic cloves, minced
- 3 tbsp butter
- 1 serrano pepper, chopped
- 1 cup beef broth
- 1 tsp ground ginger
- 2 tsp ground coriander
- Salt and pepper to taste
- ¾ tsp cumin
- ¼ tsp cayenne pepper
- ½ tsp turmeric

Directions:
1. Melt butter on Sauté. Add onion and cook for 3 minutes until soft. Stir in ginger, coriander, salt, pepper, cumin, cayenne pepper, turmeric and garlic and cook for 2 more minutes. Add pork and cook until browned. Pour broth and add serrano pepper, peas, and tomatoes. Seal the lid and cook for 30 minutes on Meat/Stew on High. When ready, release the pressure naturally for 10 minutes. Carefully unlock the lid. Serve immediately.

Sweet & Spicy Pork Ribs

Servings: 4 | Cooking Time: 50 Minutes

Ingredients:
- 3 lb pork baby back ribs
- 2 tbsp olive oil
- ¼ tsp ground coriander
- 1 tsp garlic powder
- 2 tsp cayenne pepper
- ½ cup orange marmalade
- 2 tbsp ketchup
- 2 tbsp soy sauce
- Salt and pepper to taste

Directions:
1. Trim the ribs of excess fat and cut them into individual bones. In a bowl, combine olive oil, ground coriander, garlic powder, cayenne pepper, salt, and pepper and mix well. Add in the ribs and toss to coat. Transfer them to the Instant Pot and pour in 1 cup of water. Seal the lid, select Manual, and cook for 20 minutes on High.

2. When done, release the pressure naturally for 10 minutes. In a bowl, whisk together the ketchup, orange marmalade, and soy sauce until well combined. Transfer the ribs to a baking tray. Select Sauté and pour the marmalade mixture into the pot. Cook until the sauce has thickened to obtain a glaze texture, about 4-5 minutes. Brush the ribs with some glaze and place under a preheated broiler for 5 minutes or until charred and sticky. Serve the ribs with the remaining glaze.

Eggplant & Beef Stew With Parmesan

Servings: 6 | Cooking Time: 70 Minutes

Ingredients:
- 9 oz beef neck, cut into bite-sized pieces
- 2 cups fire-roasted tomatoes
- 1 eggplant, chopped
- ½ tbsp fresh green peas
- 1 tbsp cayenne pepper
- 1 tbsp beef broth
- 4 tbsp olive oil
- 2 tbsp tomato paste
- 1 tbsp ground chili pepper
- ½ tsp salt
- Parmesan, for garnish

Directions:
1. Rub the meat with salt, cayenne, and chili pepper. Grease the Instant Pot with oil and brown the meat for 5-7 minutes or until golden on Sauté. Add tomatoes, eggplant, green peas, broth, and tomato paste and seal the lid. Cook on Meat/Stew for 40 minutes on High. Do a natural release for 10 minutes. Carefully unlock the lid. Serve warm sprinkled with grated Parmesan cheese.

Caribean-style Pork With Mango Sauce

Servings: 6 | Cooking Time: 70 Minutes

Ingredients:
- 1 ½ tsp onion powder
- 1 tsp dried thyme
- Salt and pepper to taste
- 1 tsp cayenne pepper
- 1 tsp ground allspice
- ½ tsp ground nutmeg
- ½ tsp ground cinnamon
- 2 lb pork shoulder
- 1 mango, cut into chunks
- 1 tbsp olive oil
- ½ cup water
- 2 tbsp cilantro, minced

Directions:

1. In a bowl, combine onion, thyme, allspice, cinnamon, pepper, sea salt, cayenne, and nutmeg. Coat the pork with olive oil. Season with seasoning mixture. Warm oil on Sauté in your Instant Pot. Add in the pork and cook for 5 minutes until browned completely. To the pot, add water and mango chunks. Seal the lid, press Meat/Stew, and cook on High Pressure for 45 minutes.

2. Release the pressure naturally for 10 minutes. Transfer the pork to a cutting board to cool. To make the sauce, pour the cooking liquid into a food processor and pulse until smooth. Shred the pork and arrange it on a serving platter. Serve topped with mango salsa and cilantro.

Veal Chops With Greek Yogurt

Servings: 4 | Cooking Time: 60 Minutes

Ingredients:
- 2 lb boneless veal shoulder, cubed
- 3 tomatoes, chopped
- 2 tbsp flour
- 3 tbsp butter
- 1 tbsp cayenne pepper
- 1 tsp salt
- 1 tbsp parsley, chopped
- 1 cup Greek yogurt
- 1 pide bread

Directions:

1. Grease the bottom of the inner pot with 1 tbsp of butter. Make a layer with veal pieces and Pour water to cover. Season with salt and seal the lid. Cook on High Pressure for 45 minutes. Do a quick release.

2. Melt the remaining butter in a skillet. Add the cayenne pepper and flour and briefly stir-fry, about 2 minutes. Slice pide bread and arrange on a serving plate. Place the meat and tomatoes on top. Drizzle with cayenne pepper, Top with yogurt and sprinkle with parsley to serve.

Cilantro Pork With Avocado

Servings: 4 | Cooking Time: 45 Minutes + Marinating Time

Ingredients:
- 1 lb pork tenderloin, cut into strips
- 3 garlic cloves, chopped
- ½ tsp oregano
- ½ tsp ground cumin
- 1 tbsp Hungarian paprika
- 2 tbsp olive oil
- 2 cups chicken stock
- Salt and pepper to taste
- 1 avocado, sliced
- 2 tbsp cilantro, chopped

Directions:

1. Mix garlic, oregano, cumin, paprika, salt, and pepper in a bowl. Add in pork strips and toss to coat. Let marinate for 30 minutes in the fridge. Warm the olive oil in your Instant Pot on Sauté. Place the strips in the pot and sauté for 10 minutes. Stir in chicken stock and seal the lid. Select Manual and cook for 15 minutes on High pressure.

2. When done, allow a natural release for 10 minutes, then perform a quick pressure release, and unlock the lid. Scatter with cilantro. Serve topped with avocado slices.

Butternut Squash & Beef Stew

Servings: 6 | Cooking Time: 40 Minutes

Ingredients:
- 2 lb stew beef, cut into 1-inch chunks
- ½ butternut pumpkin, chopped
- 2 tbsp canola oil
- 1 cup red wine
- 1 onion, chopped
- 1 tsp garlic powder
- 1 tsp salt
- 3 whole cloves
- 1 bay leaf
- 3 carrots, chopped
- 2 tbsp cornstarch
- 3 tbsp water

Directions:
1. Warm oil on Sauté. Brown the beef for 5 minutes on each side. Deglaze the pot with wine, scrape the bottom to get rid of any browned beef bits. Add in onion, salt, bay leaf, cloves, and garlic powder. Seal the lid, press Meat/Stew, and cook on High for 15 minutes. Release the pressure quickly. Add in pumpkin and carrots without stirring.
2. Seal the lid.Cook on High Pressure for 5 minutes. Release the pressure quickly. In a bowl, mix water and cornstarch until cornstarch dissolves completely and mix into the stew. Allow to simmer on Sauté for 5 minutes until you attain the desired thickness.

Thyme Pork Loin With Apples & Daikon

Servings: 4 | Cooking Time: 40 Minutes

Ingredients:
- 1 lb pork loin, cubed
- 1 onion, diced
- 1 daikon, chopped
- 1 cup vegetable broth
- ½ cup white wine
- 2 apples, peeled and diced
- ½ cup sliced leeks
- 1 tbsp vegetable oil
- 1 celery stalk, diced
- 2 tbsp dried parsley
- ¼ tsp thyme
- ½ tsp cumin
- ¼ tsp lemon zest
- Salt and pepper to taste

Directions:
1. Heat oil on Sauté. Add pork and cook for 6 minutes until browned. Add the onion and cook for 2 more minutes. Stir in daikon, broth, wine, leeks, celery, parsley, thyme, cumin, lemon zest, salt, and pepper. Seal the lid and cook for 15 minutes on Pressure Cook. Release the pressure quickly. Stir in apples, seal the lid again, and cook on High for another 5 minutes. Do a quick release. Carefully unlock the lid. Serve warm.

Green Pea & Beef Ragout

Servings: 4 | Cooking Time: 25 Minutes

Ingredients:
- 2 lb beef, tender cuts, cut into bits
- 2 cups green peas
- 1 onion, diced
- 1 tomato, diced
- 3 cups beef broth
- ½ cup tomato paste
- 1 tsp cayenne pepper
- 1 tbsp flour
- 1 tsp salt
- ½ tsp dried thyme
- ½ tsp red pepper flakes

Directions:
1. Add beef, green peas, onion, tomato, broth, tomato paste, cayenne pepper, flour, salt, thyme, and red pepper flakes to the Instant Pot. Seal the lid, press Manual/Pressure Cook and cook for 10 minutes on High Pressure. When done, release the steam naturally for 10 minutes. Serve.

Creamy Beef & Cauliflower Chili

Servings: 6 | Cooking Time: 20 Minutes

Ingredients:
- 1 lb beef stew meat
- 4 oz cauliflower, chopped
- 1 onion, chopped
- 2 cups beef broth
- 2 cups heavy cream
- 1 tsp Italian seasoning
- 1 tsp salt
- ½ tsp chili pepper

Directions:
1. Add beef, cauliflower, onion, broth, heavy cream,

Italian seasoning, salt, and chili pepper to your Instant Pot. Pour in 1 cup water. Seal the lid and cook on High Pressure for 15 minutes. When ready, do a quick release and serve.

Calf's Liver Venetian-style

Servings: 2 | Cooking Time: 55 Minutes

Ingredients:
- 1 lb calf's liver, rinsed
- 3 tbsp olive oil
- 2 garlic cloves, crushed
- 1 tbsp mint, chopped
- ½ tsp cayenne pepper
- ½ tsp Italian seasoning

Directions:
1. In a bowl, mix oil, garlic, mint, cayenne, and Italian seasoning. Brush the liver and chill for 30 minutes. Remove from the fridge and pat dry with paper. Place the liver into the inner pot. Seal the lid and cook on High Pressure for 5 minutes. When ready, release the steam naturally for about 10 minutes.

Ranch Potatoes With Ham

Servings: 4 | Cooking Time: 20 Minutes

Ingredients:
- 1 lb Yukon gold potatoes, quartered
- 4 oz cooked ham, chopped
- 1 tsp garlic powder
- 2 tsp chives, chopped
- Salt to taste
- 1/3 cup Ranch dressing

Directions:
1. Cover potatoes with salted water in your Instant Pot and seal the lid. Select Manual and cook for 7 minutes on High pressure.
2. When done, perform a quick pressure release and unlock the lid. Drain the potatoes and transfer to a bowl. Stir in ranch dressing, garlic powder, and ham. Sprinkle with chives and serve.

Smoky Shredded Pork With White Beans

Servings: 4 | Cooking Time: 65 Minutes

Ingredients:
- 2 lb pork shoulder, halved
- 2 tbsp vegetable oil
- 1 onion, chopped
- 1 cup vegetable broth
- 2 tbsp liquid smoke
- Salt and pepper to taste
- 1 cup cooked white beans
- 2 tbsp parsley, chopped

Directions:
1. Warm the vegetable oil in your Instant Pot on Sauté. Place in onion and cook for 3 minutes. Sprinkle pork shoulder with salt and pepper, add it to the pot and brown for 5 minutes on all sides. Pour in vegetable broth and liquid smoke and scrape any brown bits from the bottom. Seal the lid, select Manual, and cook for 35 minutes on High.
2. When ready, allow a natural release for 10 minutes, then perform a quick pressure release, and unlock the lid. Remove pork and shred it. Stir white beans in the pot and put shredded pork back. Top with parsley and serve.

Spicy Garlic Pork

Servings: 4 | Cooking Time: 45 Minutes

Ingredients:
- 1 lb pork shoulder
- 2 tbsp olive oil
- 3 Jalapeño peppers, minced
- 1 tsp ground cumin
- 1 large onion, chopped
- 2 garlic cloves, crushed
- 3 cups beef broth
- Salt and pepper to taste

Directions:
1. Heat oil on Sauté in your Instant Pot and cook the jalapeño peppers for 3 minutes. Add in cumin, salt, pepper, garlic, and onion and stir-fry for another 2 minutes until soft. Add in the pork shoulder, and beef broth. Seal the lid, and cook on Meat/Stew for 30 minutes on High. Release the pressure quickly and serve hot.

Pulled Pork

Servings:8 | Cooking Time: 70 Minutes

Ingredients:
- ½ boneless pork shoulder, quartered
- 2 teaspoons salt
- 1 teaspoon ground black pepper
- 2 tablespoons olive oil
- 2 cups beef broth

Directions:
1. Season all sides of pork with salt and pepper.
2. Press the Sauté button on the Instant Pot and heat oil. Place pork in pot. Sear meat for 5 minutes, making sure to get each side.
3. Add broth to pot. Press the Cancel button. Lock lid.
4. Press the Manual or Pressure Cook button and adjust time to 65 minutes. When timer beeps, let pressure release naturally for 10 minutes. Quick-release any additional pressure until float valve drops. Unlock lid.
5. Remove a few ladles of liquid from pot, as most is just fat rendered from pork.
6. Using two forks, shred pork and incorporate juices. Remove any additional unwanted liquid. Serve warm.

Beef Short Ribs With Asparagus Sauce

Servings: 6 | Cooking Time: 1 Hour 15 Minutes

Ingredients:
- 3 lb boneless beef short ribs, cut into pieces
- Salt and pepper to taste
- 3 tbsp olive oil
- 1 onion, diced
- 1 cup dry red wine
- 1 tbsp tomato puree
- 2 carrots, chopped
- 2 garlic cloves, minced
- 5 sprigs parsley, chopped
- 2 sprigs rosemary, chopped
- 3 sprigs oregano, chopped
- 4 cups beef stock
- 10 oz mushrooms, quartered
- 1 bunch asparagus, chopped
- 1 tbsp cornstarch

Directions:
1. Season the ribs with black pepper and salt. Warm oil on Sauté. In batches, add the short ribs to the oil and cook for 3 to 5 minutes on each side until browned. Set aside. Add onion and Sauté for 4 minutes until soft. Add tomato puree and red wine into the pot to deglaze, scrape the bottom to get rid of any browned beef bits. Cook for 2 minutes until wine reduces slightly. Return the ribs to the pot and top with carrots, oregano, rosemary, and garlic. Add in stock and press Cancel.
2. Seal the lid, press Meat/Stew, and cook on High for 35 minutes. Release pressure naturally for 10 minutes. Transfer ribs to a plate. Strain and get rid of herbs and vegetables, and return cooking stock to the inner pot. Add mushrooms and asparagus to the broth. Press Sauté and cook for 2 to 4 minutes until soft.
3. In a bowl, mix ¼ cup cold water and cornstarch until cornstarch dissolves completely. Add the cornstarch mixture into the broth as you stir for 1-3 minutes until the broth thickens slightly. Season the sauce with black pepper and salt. Pour the sauce over ribs, add chopped parsley for garnish before serving.

Pork Medallions With Porcini Sauce

Servings: 4 | Cooking Time: 60 Minutes

Ingredients:
- 1 oz dried porcini mushrooms
- 4 boneless pork loin chops
- ½ cup dry Marsala wine
- 1 garlic clove, minced
- 1 tbsp paprika
- ½ tsp rosemary
- 1 onion, sliced
- 2 tbsp butter
- Salt and pepper to taste
- 2 tbsp chopped parsley

Directions:
1. Cover the porcini mushrooms with 1 cup of boiling water in a bowl and let soak for 10-15 minutes. Sprinkle pork chops with paprika, salt, and pepper. Melt butter in your Instant Pot on Sauté. Place the pork chops in the pot and sear for 6 minutes on all sides. Set aside.
2. Add onion and garlic to the pot and cook for 3 minutes. Put pork on top along with Marsala wine, rosemary, and porcini mushrooms with the water. Seal the lid, select Manual, and cook for 15 minutes on High pressure. When over, allow a natural release for 10 minutes and unlock the lid. Garnish with parsley and serve.

Chapter 6 Fish & Seafood

Chapter 6 Fish & Seafood

Chili Steamed Catfish

Servings: 4 | Cooking Time: 70 Minutes

Ingredients:
- 1 lb flathead catfish
- 1 cup orange juice
- ¼ cup lemon juice
- ½ cup olive oil
- 1 tbsp dried thyme
- 1 tbsp dried rosemary
- 1 tsp chili flakes
- 1 tsp sea salt

Directions:
1. In a bowl, mix orange juice, lemon juice, olive oil, thyme, rosemary, chili flakes, and salt. Brush the fish with the mixture and refrigerate for 30 minutes. Remove from the fridge, drain, and reserve the marinade. Insert a trivet in the pot. Pour in 1 cup of water and marinade. Place the fish onto the top. Seal the lid and cook on High Pressure for 10 minutes. Do a quick release. Serve immediately.

Shrimp Boil With Chorizo Sausages

Servings: 4 | Cooking Time: 15 Minutes

Ingredients:
- 3 red potatoes
- 3 ears corn, cut into rounds
- 1 cup white wine
- 4 chorizo sausages, chopped
- 1 lb shrimp, deveined
- 2 tbsp of seafood seasoning
- Salt to taste
- 1 lemon, cut into wedges
- ¼ cup butter, melted

Directions:
1. Add potatoes, corn, wine, chorizo, shrimp, seafood seasoning, and salt. Do not stir. Add in 2 cups of water. Seal the lid and cook for 2 minutes on High Pressure. Release the pressure quickly. Drain the mix-ture through a colander. Transfer to a plate. Serve with melted butter and lemon wedges.

Beer-steamed Mussels

Servings: 4 | Cooking Time: 15 Minutes

Ingredients:
- 3 lb mussels, debearded
- 4 tbsp butter
- 1 shallot, chopped
- 2 garlic cloves, minced
- 2 tbsp parsley, chopped
- 1 cup beer
- 1 cup chicken stock

Directions:
1. Melt butter in your Instant Pot on Sauté. Add in shallot and garlic and cook for 2 minutes. Stir in beer and cook for 1 minute. Mix in stock and mussels and seal the lid.
2. Select Manual and cook for 3 minutes on High pressure. Once ready, perform a quick pressure release. Discard unopened mussels. Serve sprinkled with parsley.

Salmon & Broccoli Salad

Servings: 2 | Cooking Time: 15 Minutes

Ingredients:
- 2 salmon fillet
- 8 oz broccoli
- 2 mini bell peppers, chopped
- Salt and pepper to taste
- ½ lemon, juiced
- 2 tbsp olive oil
- 1 gem lettuce, torn

Directions:
1. Pour 1 cup of water into your Instant Pot and fit in a trivet. Chop broccoli into florets and transfer to a greased baking dish with the peppers. Add in the salmon and place the dish on the trivet; sprinkle with salt and pepper.
2. Seal the lid and cook for 5 minutes on Steam. When ready, perform a quick pressure release. Place the lettuce in a serving bowl, add in broccoli, peppers, olive oil, lemon juice, and salt. Top with the salmon and serve.

Seafood & Fish Stew

Servings: 6 | Cooking Time: 25 Minutes

Ingredients:
- 2 lb different fish and seafood
- 3 tbsp olive oil
- 2 onions, peeled, chopped
- 2 carrots, grated
- 2 tbsp parsley, chopped
- 2 garlic cloves, crushed
- 3 cups water
- 1 tsp sea salt

Directions:
1. Heat olive oil on Sauté. Stir-fry onions and garlic for 3-4 minutes, or until translucent. Add carrots, fish and seafood, parsley, water, and salt. Seal the lid, and cook on High Pressure for 10 minutes. Do a quick release. Serve.

Cheesy Shrimp Scampi

Servings: 4 | Cooking Time: 10 Minutes

Ingredients:
- 1 lb shrimp, deveined
- 2 tbsp olive oil
- 1 clove garlic, minced
- 1 tbsp tomato paste
- 10 oz canned tomatoes, diced
- ½ cup dry white wine
- 1 tsp red chili pepper
- 1 tbsp parsley, chopped
- Salt and pepper to taste
- 1 cup Grana Padano, grated

Directions:
1. Warm the olive oil in your Instant Pot on Sauté. Add in garlic and cook for 1 minute. Stir in shrimp, tomato paste, tomatoes, white wine, chili pepper, parsley, salt, pepper, and ¼ cup of water and seal the lid. Select Manual and cook for 3 minutes on High pressure. Once done, perform a quick pressure release and unlock the lid. Serve garnished with Grana Padano cheese.

White Wine Oysters

Servings: 4 | Cooking Time: 10 Minutes

Ingredients:
- 2 lb in-shell oysters, cleaned
- 1 cup vegetable broth
- 4 tbsp white wine
- 2 tbsp thyme, chopped
- 1 garlic clove, minced
- Salt and pepper to taste
- 4 tbsp butter, melted

Directions:
1. Place the vegetable broth, oysters, white wine, garlic, salt, and pepper in your Instant Pot and seal the lid. Select Manual and cook for 3 minutes on High pressure. Once done, perform a quick pressure release and unlock the lid. Drain the oysters, drizzle with the melted butter, and top with thyme to serve.

Pistachio-parm–crusted Cod

Servings:2 | Cooking Time: 7 Minutes

Ingredients:
- 2 tablespoons unsalted butter, melted
- 1 tablespoon panko bread crumbs
- 2 tablespoons chopped unsalted pistachios
- 2 tablespoons grated Parmesan cheese
- ¼ teaspoon salt
- 2 cod fillets
- 1 cup water

Directions:
1. In a small bowl, combine butter, bread crumbs, pistachios, cheese, and salt to form a thick paste.
2. Pat cod fillets dry with a paper towel. Rub paste on top of each fillet and place in steamer basket.
3. Add water to the Instant Pot and insert steam rack. Place steamer basket on steam rack. Lock lid.
4. Press the Manual or Pressure Cook button and adjust time to 5 minutes. When timer beeps, quick-release the pressure until float valve drops. Unlock lid.
5. Line a baking sheet with parchment paper. Transfer fillets to prepared baking sheet. Broil approximately 1–2 minutes until tops are browned.
6. Remove from heat and serve hot.

Easy Seafood Paella

Servings: 4 | Cooking Time: 20 Minutes

Ingredients:
- 1 cup tiger prawns, peeled and deveined
- 1 lb mussels, cleaned and debearded
- ½ tsp guindilla (cayenne pepper)
- ½ lb clams
- 2 tbsp olive oil
- 1 onion, chopped
- 2 garlic cloves, minced
- 1 red bell pepper, chopped
- 1 cup rice
- 2 cups clam juice
- ¾ cup green peas, frozen
- 1 tbsp parsley, chopped
- 1 tbsp turmeric
- 1 whole lemon, quartered

Directions:
1. Warm the olive oil in your Instant Pot on Sauté. Add in prawns, red pepper, onion, and garlic and cook for 3 minutes. Stir in rice for 1 minute and pour in clam juice, turmeric, mussels, and clams. Seal the lid, select Manual, and cook for 5 minutes on High pressure. When ready, perform a quick pressure release and unlock the lid. Stir in green peas and guindilla for 3-4 minutes. Top with lemon quarters and parsley. Serve immediately.

Littleneck Clams In Garlic Wine Broth

Servings:4 | Cooking Time: 8 Minutes

Ingredients:
- 2 pounds fresh littleneck clams, cleaned and debearded
- 2 tablespoons olive oil
- 1 medium yellow onion, peeled and diced
- 4 cloves garlic, peeled and minced
- ½ cup dry white wine
- ½ cup vegetable broth
- ½ teaspoon salt
- 4 tablespoons chopped fresh parsley

Directions:
1. Let clams soak in water 30 minutes. Rinse several times. This will help purge any sand trapped in the shells.
2. Press the Sauté button on the Instant Pot and heat oil. Add onion and sauté 3–5 minutes until translucent. Add garlic and cook an additional 1 minute. Stir in wine, broth, and salt and let cook 2 minutes. Press the Cancel button.
3. Insert steamer basket. Place clams in basket. Lock lid.
4. Press the Manual or Pressure Cook button and adjust time to 0 minutes. When timer beeps, quick-release pressure until float valve drops. Unlock lid.
5. Remove clams and discard any that haven't opened. Transfer clams to four bowls and pour liquid from the Instant Pot equally among bowls. Garnish each bowl with 1 tablespoon parsley. Serve immediately.

Smoky Salmon With Garlic Mayo Sauce

Servings: 6 | Cooking Time: 25 Minutes

Ingredients:
- 2 lb salmon fillets
- ½ cup mayonnaise
- 1 tbsp lemon juice
- 2 garlic cloves, minced
- 1 tsp dill
- 1 tsp smoked paprika
- 2 tbsp olive oil
- 2 tbsp chives, chopped
- Salt and pepper to taste

Directions:
1. Mix the mayonnaise, smoked paprika, lemon juice, garlic, and dill in a bowl. Set aside. Sprinkle salmon with salt and pepper. Warm the olive oil in your Instant Pot on Sauté. Place in salmon and cook for 3-4 minutes per side. Spread the mayonnaise mixture on the salmon and cook for 5 minutes, turning once. Serve topped with chives.

Paprika Catfish With Fresh Tarragon

Servings:2 | Cooking Time: 3 Minutes

Ingredients:
- 1 can diced tomatoes, including juice
- 2 teaspoons dried minced onion
- ¼ teaspoon onion powder
- 1 teaspoon dried minced garlic
- ¼ teaspoon garlic powder
- 2 teaspoons smoked paprika
- 1 tablespoon chopped fresh tarragon
- 1 medium green bell pepper, seeded and diced
- 1 stalk celery, finely diced
- 1 teaspoon salt
- ¼ teaspoon ground black pepper
- 1 pound catfish fillets, rinsed and cut into bite-sized pieces

Directions:
1. Add all ingredients except fish to the Instant Pot and stir to mix. Once mixed, add the fish on top. Lock lid.
2. Press the Manual button and adjust time to 3 minutes. When timer beeps, quick-release pressure until float valve drops and then unlock lid.
3. Transfer all ingredients to a serving bowl. Serve

warm.

Herby Trout With Farro & Green Beans

Servings: 4 | Cooking Time: 20 Minutes

Ingredients:
- 1 cup farro
- 2 cups water
- 4 skinless trout fillets
- 8 oz green beans
- 1 tbsp olive oil
- Salt and pepper to taste
- 4 tbsp melted butter
- ½ tbsp sugar
- ½ tbsp lemon juice
- ½ tsp dried rosemary
- 2 garlic cloves, minced
- ½ tsp dried thyme

Directions:
1. Pour the farro and water into the pot and mix with green beans and olive oil. Season with salt and black pepper. In another bowl, mix the remaining black pepper and salt, butter, sugar, lemon juice, rosemary, garlic, and thyme.
2. Coat the trout with the buttery herb sauce. Insert a trivet in the pot and lay the trout fillets on the trivet. Seal the lid and cook on High Pressure for 12 minutes. Do a quick release and serve immediately.

Steamed Shrimp And Asparagus

Servings:2 | Cooking Time: 1 Minute

Ingredients:
- 1 cup water
- 1 bunch asparagus
- 1 teaspoon sea salt, divided
- 1 pound shrimp, peeled and deveined
- ½ lemon
- 2 tablespoons butter, cut into 2 pats

Directions:
1. Pour water into Instant Pot. Insert trivet. Place steamer basket onto trivet.
2. Prepare asparagus by finding the natural snap point on the stalks and discarding the woody ends.
3. Spread the asparagus on the bottom of the steamer basket. Sprinkle with ½ teaspoon salt. Add the shrimp. Squeeze lemon into the Instant Pot, then sprinkle

shrimp with remaining ½ teaspoon salt. Place pats of butter on shrimp. Lock lid.

4. Press the Manual button and adjust time to 1 minute. When the timer beeps, quick-release the pressure until the float valve drops and then unlock lid.

5. Transfer shrimp and asparagus to a platter and serve.

Steamed Clams

Servings:4 | Cooking Time: 10 Minutes

Ingredients:
- 2 pounds fresh clams, rinsed and purged
- 1 tablespoon olive oil
- 1 small white onion, peeled and diced
- 1 clove garlic, quartered
- ½ cup chardonnay
- ½ cup water

Directions:
1. Place clams in the steamer basket. Set aside.
2. Press the Sauté button on Instant Pot. Heat olive oil. Add onion and sauté 3–5 minutes until translucent. Add garlic and cook another minute. Pour in white wine and water. Insert steamer basket. Lock lid.
3. Press the Manual button and adjust time to 4 minutes. When the timer beeps, quick-release pressure until lid unlocks.
4. Transfer clams to four serving bowls and top with a generous scoop of cooking liquid.

Vietnamese Fish & Noodle Soup

Servings: 6 | Cooking Time: 32 Minutes

Ingredients:
- 2 tbsp sesame oil
- 1 lb snapper fillets, chopped
- 12 oz squid
- 5 oz rice noodles
- ¼ cup soy sauce
- ¼ tsp thyme
- ½ tbsp cilantro, chopped
- 1 tsp chili flakes
- 1 garlic clove, sliced
- 1 onion, thinly sliced
- Salt and pepper to taste

Directions:
1. Heat the sesame oil in your Instant Pot on Sauté. Add in onion, garlic, salt, and pepper and cook for 2

minutes. Stir in fish, squid, chili flakes, and thyme and sauté for 5-6 minutes. Pour in soy sauce and 5 cups of water and seal the lid. Select Manual and cook for 10 minutes.

2. Once ready, perform a quick pressure release. Press Sauté and add in the rice noodles. Cook for 3-4 minutes until just tender. Ladle into bowls and serve scattered cilantro.

Paprika Salmon With Dill Sauce

Servings: 2 | Cooking Time: 15 Minutes

Ingredients:
- 2 salmon fillets
- ¼ tsp paprika
- Salt and pepper to taste
- ¼ cup fresh dill
- Juice from ½ lemon
- Sea salt to taste
- ¼ cup olive oil

Directions:
1. In a food processor, blend the olive oil, lemon juice, dill, and seas salt until creamy; reserve. To the cooker, add 1 cup water and place a steamer basket. Arrange salmon fillets skin-side down on the steamer basket. Sprinkle the salmon with paprika, salt, and pepper. Seal the lid and cook for 3 minutes on High Pressure. Release the pressure quickly. Top the fillets with dill sauce to serve.

Dilled Salmon Fillets

Servings: 4 | Cooking Time: 25 Minutes

Ingredients:
- 4 salmon fillets
- 1 cup lemon juice
- 2 tbsp butter, softened
- 2 tbsp dill
- Salt and pepper to taste

Directions:
1. Sprinkle the fillets with salt and pepper. Insert the steamer tray and place the salmon on top. Pour in the lemon juice and 2 cups of water. Seal the lid. Cook on Steam for 5 minutes on High.
2. Release the pressure naturally for 10 minutes. Set aside the salmon and discard the liquid. Wipe the pot clean and press Sauté. Add butter and briefly brown the fillets on both sides, about 3-4 minutes. Sprinkle with dill.

Dijon Catfish Fillets With White Wine

Servings: 3 | Cooking Time: 15 Minutes + Cooling Time

Ingredients:
- 1 lb catfish fillets
- 1 lemon, juiced
- ½ cup parsley, chopped
- 2 garlic cloves, crushed
- 1 onion, finely chopped
- 1 tbsp dill, chopped
- 1 tbsp rosemary, chopped
- 2 cups white wine
- 2 tbsp Dijon mustard
- 1 cup extra virgin olive oil

Directions:
1. In a bowl, mix lemon juice, parsley, garlic, onion, dill, rosemary, wine, mustard, and oil. Stir well. Submerge the fillets and cover with a tight lid. Refrigerate for 1 hour. Insert a trivet in the Instant Pot. Remove the fish from the fridge and place it on the rack. Pour in 1 cup of water and marinade. Seal the lid. Cook on Steam for 8 minutes on High. Release the pressure quickly. Serve immediately.

Steamed Salmon Over Creamy Polenta

Servings: 4 | Cooking Time: 30 Minutes

Ingredients:
- 4 salmon fillets, skin removed
- 1 cup corn grits polenta
- ½ cup coconut milk
- 3 cups chicken stock
- 3 tbsp butter
- Salt to taste
- 3 tbsp Cajun seasoning
- 1 tbsp sugar

Directions:
1. Combine polenta, milk, chicken stock, butter, and salt in the pot. In a bowl, mix Cajun seasoning, sugar, and salt. Oil the fillets with cooking spray and brush with the spice mixture. Insert a trivet in the pot and arrange the fillets on top. Seal the lid and cook on High Pressure for 9 minutes. Do a natural pressure release for 10 minutes.

Salmon Steaks With Garlic & Lemon

Servings: 3 | Cooking Time: 60 Minutes

Ingredients:
- 1 lb salmon steaks
- 1 tsp garlic powder
- 2 tbsp olive oil
- Salt and pepper to taste
- ¼ cup lemon juice

Directions:
1. In a bowl, mix garlic powder, olive oil, salt, lemon juice, and pepper. Pour the mixture into a Ziploc bag along with the salmon. Seal the bag and shake to coat well. Refrigerate for 30 minutes. Pour in 1 cup of water in the Instant Pot and insert the trivet. Remove the fish from the Ziploc bag and place it on top. Reserve the marinade. Seal the lid and select Steam.
2. Cook for 15 minutes on High. When ready, do a quick release and remove the steaks. Discard the liquid. Wipe clean the pot. Pour in the marinade and hit Sauté. Cook for 3-4 minutes. Serve the salmon drizzled with the sauce.

Basil Clams With Garlic & White Wine

Servings: 4 | Cooking Time: 15 Minutes

Ingredients:
- 1 lb clams, scrubbed
- 2 tbsp butter
- 4 green garlic, chopped
- 1 tbsp lemon juice
- ½ cup white wine
- ½ cup chicken stock
- Salt and pepper to taste
- 2 tbsp basil, chopped

Directions:
1. Melt the butter in your Instant Pot on Sauté. Add in the garlic and clams and cook for 3-4 minutes. Stir in lemon juice and chicken stock, white wine, salt, and pepper and seal the lid. Select Manual and cook for 3 minutes on High pressure. Once done, perform a quick pressure release and unlock the lid. Discard unopened clams. Serve topped with basil.

Thyme For Lemon-butter Sea Bass

Servings:2 | Cooking Time: 7 Minutes

Ingredients:
- 2 tablespoons unsalted butter, melted
- 1 tablespoon lemon juice
- 2 teaspoons fresh thyme leaves
- ¼ cup Italian bread crumbs
- 2 sea bass fillets
- ½ teaspoon salt
- ¼ teaspoon ground black pepper
- 1 cup water

Directions:
1. In a small bowl, combine butter, lemon juice, thyme, and bread crumbs to form a thick paste.
2. Pat sea bass fillets dry with a paper towel. Season sea bass with salt and pepper. Press paste on top of each fillet and place in steamer basket.
3. Add water to the Instant Pot and insert steam rack. Place basket on steam rack. Lock lid.
4. Press the Manual or Pressure Cook button and adjust time to 5 minutes. When timer beeps, quick-release pressure until float valve drops. Unlock lid.
5. Line a baking sheet with parchment paper. Transfer fillets to prepared baking sheet. Broil approximately 1–2 minutes until tops are browned.
6. Remove from heat. Serve warm.

Citrus Smelt With Okra & Cherry Tomatoes

Servings: 4 | Cooking Time: 30 Minutes + Cooling Time

Ingredients:
- 1 lb fresh smelt, cleaned, heads removed
- 1 cup extra virgin olive oil
- ½ cup lemon juice
- ¼ cup orange juice
- 1 tbsp Dijon mustard
- 1 tsp rosemary, chopped
- 4 tbsp vegetable oil
- 2 garlic cloves, crushed
- 1 tsp sea salt
- 5 oz okra
- 1 carrot, chopped
- ¼ cup green peas
- 5 oz cherry tomatoes, halved
- 1 cup fish stock

Directions:
1. In a bowl, mix olive oil, lemon and orange juices, Dijon mustard, garlic, salt, and rosemary. Stir well and submerge fish in this mixture. Refrigerate for 1 hour. Heat the vegetable oil on Sauté and stir-fry carrot, peas, cherry tomatoes, and okra for 10 minutes. Add in the fish stock.
2. Place a trivet over the mixture and lower the fish onto the trivet. Pour in the marinade. Seal the lid and cook on Manual for 8 minutes on High. When done, do a quick release. Serve the smelt drizzled with the cooking sauce.

Mackerel With Potatoes & Spinach

Servings: 4 | Cooking Time: 20 Minutes

Ingredients:
- 4 mackerels, skin on
- 1 lb spinach, torn
- 5 potatoes, peeled, chopped
- 3 tbsp olive oil
- 2 garlic cloves, crushed
- 2 tbsp mint leaves, chopped
- 1 lemon, juiced
- Sea salt to taste

Directions:
1. Heat 2 tbsp of the olive oil on Sauté. Stir-fry garlic for 1 minute. Stir in spinach and salt and cook for 4-5 minutes until wilted; set aside. Make a layer of potatoes in the pot. Top with fish and drizzle with lemon juice, remaining olive oil, and salt. Pour in 1 cup of water, seal the lid, and cook on Steam for 7 minutes on High. When ready, do a quick release. Carefully unlock the lid. Plate the fish and potatoes with spinach and serve topped with mint leaves.

Baja Fish Street Tacos

Servings:4 | Cooking Time: 3 Minutes

Ingredients:
- Slaw
- ½ cup grated red cabbage
- 2 medium limes (juice ½ lime for the slaw; cut the rest into wedges for garnish)
- 1 tablespoon olive oil
- 1 teaspoon hot sauce
- 1 tablespoon mayonnaise
- ½ teaspoon salt
- Fish
- 1 pound cod, cubed
- ½ teaspoon salt
- ½ teaspoon ground black pepper
- 1 cup water
- To Serve
- 8 soft flour street taco tortillas, warmed

Directions:
1. In a medium bowl, combine all slaw ingredients. Refrigerate covered 30 minutes or up to overnight.
2. In a large bowl, season fish with salt and pepper.
3. Add water to the Instant Pot and insert steam rack. Place steamer basket on top of steam rack. Add cod in an even row into basket. Lock lid.
4. Press the Manual or Pressure Cook button and adjust time to 3 minutes. When timer beeps, quick-release pressure until float valve drops. Unlock lid. Transfer fish to a serving dish.
5. Assemble fish tacos by adding equal amounts fish and slaw to each tortilla. Serve with lime wedges.

Lobster Risotto

Servings:4 | Cooking Time: 20 Minutes

Ingredients:
- 4 tablespoons butter
- 1 small onion, peeled and finely diced
- 2 cloves garlic, minced
- 1½ cups Arborio rice
- 1 cup chardonnay
- 3 cups vegetable broth
- ½ teaspoon lemon zest
- 3 tablespoons grated Parmesan cheese
- ½ teaspoon salt
- ¼ teaspoon ground black pepper
- Meat from 3 small lobster tails, diced
- ¼ cup chopped fresh parsley

Directions:
1. Press the Sauté button on the Instant Pot and add the butter. Heat until melted. Add onion and stir-fry for 3–5 minutes until translucent. Add garlic and rice and cook for an additional minute. Add white wine and slowly stir unlidded for 5 minutes until liquid is absorbed by the rice.
2. Add broth, lemon zest, Parmesan, salt, and pepper. Lock lid.
3. Press the Rice button. Let pressure release naturally for 10 minutes. Quick-release any additional pressure until float valve drops and then unlock lid.
4. Stir in lobster, garnish with fresh parsley, and serve warm.

Saucy Clams With Herbs

Servings: 4 | Cooking Time: 15 Minutes

Ingredients:
- 1 lb clams, scrubbed
- 2 tsp olive oil
- 2 garlic cloves, minced
- 1 onion, chopped
- 2 celery stalks, diced
- 1 bell pepper, diced
- 1 tbsp tomato paste
- 28 oz can crushed tomatoes
- ½ tsp basil
- 1 tsp rosemary
- ½ tsp oregano
- Salt and pepper to taste
- ¼ tsp chili pepper

Directions:
1. Warm the olive oil in your Instant Pot on Sauté. Place in garlic, onion, celery, and bell pepper and cook for 3-4 minutes. Add in tomato paste and cook for another 1 minute. Stir in clams, tomatoes, basil, rosemary, oregano, salt, pepper, and chili pepper and seal the lid. Select Manual and cook for 2 minutes on High pressure. Once done, perform a quick pressure release and unlock the lid. Discard unopened clams. Serve with cooked rice.

Mustard Salmon

Servings: 2 | Cooking Time: 15 Minutes

Ingredients:
- 2 salmon fillets
- Salt and pepper to taste
- 1 rosemary sprig
- 1 thyme sprig
- 1 tbsp parsley, chopped
- 1 tbsp olive oil
- 2 tsp Dijon mustard

Directions:
1. Pour 1 cup of water into your Instant Pot and fit in a trivet. Brush the salmon fillets with mustard and place it skin-side down on the rack. Top with olive oil, rosemary, thyme, and parsley. Season with salt and pepper. Seal the lid, select Manual, and cook for 5 minutes on High. Once done, perform a quick pressure release. Serve.

Seafood Traditional Spanish Paella

Servings: 4 | Cooking Time: 30 Minutes

Ingredients:
- 2 tbsp olive oil
- 1 onion, chopped
- 4 garlic cloves, minced
- ½ cup dry white wine
- 1 cup rice
- 1 ½ cups chicken stock
- 1 ½ tsp sweet paprika
- 1 tsp turmeric powder
- 1 lb small clams, scrubbed
- 1 lb prawns, deveined
- 1 red bell pepper, diced
- 1 lemon, cut into wedges

Directions:
1. Cook onion and garlic in 1 tbsp of oil on Sauté for 3 minutes. Pour in wine to deglaze, scraping the bottom of the pot of any brown. Cook for 2 minutes until the wine is reduced by half. Add in rice and broth. Stir in paprika, turmeric, and bell pepper. Seal the lid and cook on High Pressure for 10 minutes. Do a quick release. Remove to a plate and wipe the pot clean. Heat the remaining oil on Sauté. Cook clams and prawns for 6 minutes until the shrimp are pink. Discard unopened clams. Arrange seafood and lemon wedges over paella to serve.

Chapter 7 Vegan & Vegetarian

Tofu With Noodles & Peanuts

Servings: 4 | Cooking Time: 15 Minutes

Ingredients:
- 1 package tofu, cubed
- 8 oz egg noodles
- 2 bell peppers, chopped
- ¼ cup soy sauce
- ¼ cup orange juice
- 1 tbsp fresh ginger, minced
- 2 tbsp vinegar
- 1 tbsp sesame oil
- 1 tbsp sriracha
- ¼ cup roasted peanuts
- 3 scallions, chopped

Directions:
1. In the Instant Pot, mix tofu, bell peppers, orange juice, sesame oil, ginger, egg noodles, soy sauce, vinegar, and sriracha. Cover with enough water. Seal the lid and cook for 2 minutes on High Pressure. Release the pressure quickly. Divide the meal between 4 plates and top with scallions and peanuts to serve.

Macaroni And Cheese

Servings:6 | Cooking Time: 4 Minutes

Ingredients:
- 1 pound elbow macaroni
- ¼ cup milk
- 1 cup shredded sharp Cheddar
- ¼ cup ricotta cheese
- 2 tablespoons grated Parmesan cheese
- 2 tablespoons butter
- ½ teaspoon ground mustard
- 2 teaspoons salt
- ½ teaspoon ground black pepper

Directions:
1. Place macaroni in an even layer in Instant Pot. Pour enough water to come about ¼" over pasta. Lock lid.
2. Press the Manual button and adjust time to 4 minutes. When the timer beeps, let the pressure release naturally for 3 minutes. Quick-release any additional pressure until float valve drops and then unlock lid.
3. Drain any residual water. Add milk, Cheddar, ricotta, Parmesan, butter, mustard, salt, and pepper. Stir in the warmed pot until well-combined. Serve warm.

Spicy Vegetable Pilaf

Servings: 4 | Cooking Time: 40 Minutes

Ingredients:
- 3 tbsp olive oil
- 1 tbsp ginger, minced
- 1 cup onion, chopped
- 1 cup green peas
- 1 cup carrots, chopped
- 1 cup mushrooms, chopped
- 1 cup broccoli, chopped
- 1 tbsp chili powder
- ½ tbsp ground cumin
- 1 tbsp garam masala
- ½ tbsp turmeric
- 1 cup basmati rice
- 2 cups vegetable broth
- 1 tbsp lemon juice
- Salt and pepper to taste

Directions:
1. Warm 1 tbsp olive oil on Sauté. Add in onion and ginger and cook for 3 minutes. Stir in broccoli, green peas, mushrooms, and carrots and cook for 5 minutes. Stir in the turmeric, chili powder, garam masala, salt, pepper, and cumin for 1 minute. Add ¼ cup broth and scrape the bottom to get rid of any browned bits. Add the remaining broth and rice. Seal the lid and cook for 20 minutes on High Pressure. Release the pressure quickly. Drizzle with lemon juice and serve.

Stuffed Peppers With Rice & Mushrooms

Servings: 4 | Cooking Time: 40 Minutes

Ingredients:
- 4 bell peppers, seeds and stems removed
- 6 oz button mushrooms, chopped
- 1 onion, peeled, chopped
- 2 garlic cloves, minced
- 2 tbsp olive oil
- ½ cup rice
- ½ tbsp paprika
- 2 cups vegetable stock

Directions:
1. Warm the olive oil on Sauté. Add onion, garlic, and mushrooms, and stir-fry until tender for about 5 minutes. Press Cancel and set aside. In a bowl, combine rice with the mixture from the pot. Sprinkle with paprika.
2. Stuff each bell pepper with this mixture. Place them in the Instant Pot, filled side up, and pour in the stock. Seal the lid and cook on High Pressure for 15 minutes. Release the pressure naturally for about 10 minutes.

Bavarian Kale And Potatoes

Servings:4 | Cooking Time: 10 Minutes

Ingredients:
- 1 tablespoon olive oil
- 1 small onion, peeled and diced
- 1 stalk celery, diced
- 2 cloves garlic, minced
- 4 medium potatoes, peeled and diced
- 2 bunches kale, washed, deveined, and chopped
- 1½ cups vegetable broth
- 2 teaspoons salt
- ½ teaspoon ground black pepper
- ¼ teaspoon caraway seeds
- 1 tablespoon apple cider vinegar
- 4 tablespoons sour cream

Directions:
1. Press the Sauté button on Instant Pot. Heat oil. Add onion and celery and stir-fry 3–5 minutes until onions are translucent. Add garlic and cook for an additional minute. Add potatoes in an even layer. Add chopped kale in an even layer. Add broth. Lock lid.
2. Press the Manual button and adjust time to 5 minutes. Let the pressure release naturally for 10 minutes.

Quick-release any additional pressure until float valve drops and then unlock lid; then drain broth.
3. Stir in salt, pepper, caraway seeds, and vinegar; slightly mash the potatoes in the Instant Pot. Garnish each serving with 1 tablespoon sour cream.

Mighty "meat"loaf

Servings:4 | Cooking Time: 12 Minutes

Ingredients:
- 1 can cannellini beans, drained and rinsed
- 1 cup finely chopped baby bella mushrooms
- 2 small shallots, minced
- 1 large carrot, peeled and grated
- 2 garlic cloves, minced
- 2 large eggs, whisked
- 1 cup shredded mozzarella cheese
- 1 tablespoon Italian seasoning
- 1 teaspoon sea salt
- ½ teaspoon ground black pepper
- 1 cup old-fashioned oats
- 1 tablespoon Dijon mustard
- 1 can tomato sauce
- 1 cup water

Directions:
1. Add beans to a medium mixing bowl. Using the back of a wooden spoon, smash the beans against the side of the bowl until they all pop open. Add remaining ingredients except water and mix well. Form mixture into a ball and place into a greased 7-cup glass bowl. Slightly press down the top of the ball.
2. Pour 1 cup water into Instant Pot. Insert trivet. Place glass bowl onto trivet. Lock lid.
3. Press the Manual button and adjust time to 12 minutes. When timer beeps, quick-release pressure until float valve drops and then unlock lid. Remove bowl from Instant Pot and let cool for 15 minutes before serving.

Parmesan Topped Vegetable Mash

Servings: 6 | Cooking Time: 15 Minutes

Ingredients:
- 3 lb Yukon gold potatoes, chopped
- 2 cups cauliflower florets
- 1 carrot, chopped
- 1 cup Parmesan, shredded
- ¼ cup butter, melted
- ¼ cup milk
- 1 tsp salt
- 1 garlic clove, minced
- 2 tbsp parsley, chopped

Directions:
1. Into the pot, add potatoes, cauliflower, carrot and salt; cover with enough water. Seal the lid and cook on High Pressure for 10 minutes. Release the pressure quickly. Drain the vegetables and mash them with a potato masher. Add garlic, butter, and milk. Whisk until well incorporated. Top with Parmesan cheese and parsley.

Red Wine And Mushroom Risotto

Servings:4 | Cooking Time: 19 Minutes

Ingredients:
- 2 tablespoons olive oil
- 1 small yellow onion, peeled and finely diced
- 1 cup sliced baby bella mushrooms
- 2 cloves garlic, peeled and minced
- 1 ½ cups Arborio rice
- 3 cups vegetable broth, divided
- 1 cup dry red wine (cabernet sauvignon or pinot noir)
- ½ teaspoon salt
- ¼ teaspoon ground black pepper

Directions:
1. Press the Sauté button on the Instant Pot and heat oil. Add onion and mushrooms and stir-fry 3–5 minutes until onions are translucent. Add garlic and rice and cook an additional 1 minute. Add 1 cup broth and stir 2–3 minutes until it is absorbed by rice.
2. Add remaining 2 cups broth, wine, salt, and pepper. Press the Cancel button. Lock lid.
3. Press the Manual or Pressure Cook button and adjust time to 10 minutes. When timer beeps, let pressure release naturally for 10 minutes. Quick-release any additional pressure until float valve drops. Unlock lid.

4. Ladle into bowls. Serve warm.

White Bean Cassoulet

Servings:6 | Cooking Time: 45 Minutes

Ingredients:
- 1 tablespoon olive oil
- 1 medium onion, peeled and diced
- 2 cups dried cannellini beans
- 1 medium parsnip, peeled and diced small
- 2 medium carrots, peeled and diced small
- 2 stalks celery, diced
- 1 medium zucchini, diced large
- ½ teaspoon fennel seed
- ¼ teaspoon ground nutmeg
- ½ teaspoon garlic powder
- 1 teaspoon sea salt
- ½ teaspoon ground black pepper
- 2 cups vegetable broth
- 1 can diced tomatoes, including juice
- 2 sprigs rosemary

Directions:
1. Press the Sauté button on Instant Pot. Heat oil Add onion and stir-fry 3–5 minutes until onions are translucent. Add beans and toss.
2. Add a layer of diced parsnips, then a layer of carrots, and next a layer of celery. Finally, add a layer of zucchini. Sprinkle in fennel seed, nutmeg, garlic powder, salt, and pepper.
3. Gently pour in broth and canned tomatoes. Then add rosemary. Lock lid.
4. Press the Bean button and cook for the default time of 30 minutes. When timer beeps, let pressure release naturally for 10 minutes. Quick-release any additional pressure until float valve drops and then unlock lid.
5. Press the Sauté button on the Instant Pot, press the Adjust button to change the temperature to Less, and simmer bean mixture unlidded for 10 minutes to thicken. Transfer to a serving bowl and carefully toss. Discard rosemary and serve.

Mushroom & Ricotta Cheese Manicotti

Servings: 4 | Cooking Time: 35 Minutes

Ingredients:
- 6 oz button mushrooms, chopped
- 8 oz pack manicotti pasta
- 12 oz spinach, torn
- 3 oz ricotta cheese
- ¼ cup milk
- 3 oz butter
- ¼ tbsp salt
- 1 tbsp sour cream

Directions:

1. Melt butter on Sauté and add mushrooms. Cook until soft, 5 minutes. Add spinach and milk and continue to cook for 6 minutes. Stir in cheese and season with salt. Line a baking dish with parchment paper. Fill manicotti with spinach mixture. Transfer them on the baking sheet. Pour 1 cup water into the Instant Pot and insert a trivet. Lay the baking sheet on the trivet. Seal the lid and cook on High Pressure for 15 minutes. Do a quick release. Top with sour cream and serve.

Power Green Soup With Lasagna Noodles

Servings: 4 | Cooking Time: 25 Minutes

Ingredients:
- 1 tsp olive oil
- 1 cup leeks, chopped
- 2 garlic cloves minced
- 1 cup tomato paste
- 1 cup tomatoes, chopped
- 1 carrot, chopped
- ½ lb broccoli, chopped
- ¼ cup dried green lentils
- 2 tsp Italian seasoning
- Salt to taste
- 2 cups vegetable broth
- 3 lasagna noodles

Directions:

1. Warm olive oil on Sauté. Add garlic and leeks and cook for 2 minutes until soft; add tomato paste, carrot, Italian seasoning, broccoli, tomatoes, lentils, and salt. Stir in vegetable broth and lasagna noodles. Seal the lid and cook on High Pressure for 3 minutes. Release pressure naturally for 10 minutes. Divide into bowls and serve.

Turmeric Stew With Green Peas

Servings: 4 | Cooking Time: 35 Minutes

Ingredients:
- 2 cups green peas
- 1 onion, chopped
- 4 cloves garlic, minced
- 3 oz of olives, pitted
- 1 tbsp ginger, shredded
- 1 tbsp turmeric
- 1 tbsp salt
- 4 cups vegetable stock
- 3 tbsp olive oil

Directions:

1. Heat olive oil on Sauté. Stir-fry the onion and garlic for 2-3 minutes, stirring a few times. Add peas, olives, ginger, turmeric, salt, and stock and press Cancel. Seal the lid, select Manual, and cook on High Pressure for 20 minutes. Once the timer goes off, do a quick release before opening the lid. Serve with a dollop of yogurt.

One-pot Swiss Chard & Potatoes

Servings: 4 | Cooking Time: 15 Minutes

Ingredients:
- 1 lb Swiss chard, chopped
- 2 potatoes, peeled, chopped
- ¼ tsp oregano
- 1 tsp salt
- 1 tsp Italian seasoning

Directions:

1. Add Swiss chard and potatoes to the pot. Pour water to cover all and sprinkle with salt. Seal the lid and select Manual. Cook for 3 minutes on High. Release the steam naturally for 5 minutes. Transfer to a serving plate. Sprinkle with oregano and Italian seasoning and serve.

Quick Cassoulet

Servings:6 | Cooking Time: 45 Minutes

Ingredients:
- 1 tablespoon olive oil
- 1 medium yellow onion, peeled and diced
- 2 cups dried cannellini beans, rinsed and drained
- 2 medium carrots, peeled and diced small
- 1 tablespoon Italian seasoning
- 1 teaspoon garlic salt
- ½ teaspoon ground black pepper
- 2 ½ cups vegetable broth
- 1 can diced tomatoes, including juice
- 4 vegan smoked apple sausages, each cut into 4 sections

Directions:
1. Press the Sauté button on the Instant Pot and heat oil. Add onion and stir-fry 3–5 minutes until onions are translucent. Add beans and toss.
2. Add carrots, Italian seasoning, garlic salt, and pepper.
3. Gently pour in broth and diced tomatoes. Press the Cancel button. Lock lid.
4. Press the Bean button and cook for the default time of 30 minutes. When timer beeps, let pressure release naturally for 10 minutes. Quick-release any additional pressure until float valve drops. Press the Cancel button. Unlock lid. Add sausage.
5. Press the Sauté button on the Instant Pot, press the Adjust button to change the temperature to Less, and simmer bean mixture unlidded 10 minutes to thicken. Transfer to a serving bowl and carefully toss. Serve warm.

Parsnip & Cauliflower Mash With Chives

Servings: 8 | Cooking Time: 15 Minutes

Ingredients:
- 1 ½ lb parsnips, cubed
- 10 oz cauliflower florets
- 2 garlic cloves
- Salt and pepper to taste
- ¼ cup sour cream
- ¼ cup grated Parmesan
- 1 tbsp butter
- 2 tbsp minced chives

Directions:
1. In the pot, mix parsnips, garlic, 2 cups water, salt, cauliflower, and pepper. Seal the lid and cook on High Pressure for 4 minutes. Release the pressure quickly. Drain parsnips and cauliflower and return to pot. Add Parmesan, butter, and sour cream. Use a potato masher to mash until the desired consistency is attained. Top with chives and place to a serving plate. Serve.

Seasoned Black Beans

Servings:8 | Cooking Time: 45 Minutes

Ingredients:
- 1 cup dried black beans
- 1 tablespoon olive oil
- 1 small onion, peeled and diced
- 3 cloves garlic, minced
- 2 cups vegetable broth
- ¼ teaspoon ground coriander
- ½ teaspoon chili powder
- ¼ teaspoon ground cumin
- ½ teaspoon sea salt
- 2 teaspoons Italian seasoning

Directions:
1. Rinse and drain beans.
2. Press the Sauté button on Instant Pot. Heat olive oil and add onion. Stir-fry 3–5 minutes until onions are translucent. Add garlic and sauté for an additional minute. Deglaze the Instant Pot by adding broth and scraping the bottom and sides of Instant Pot.
3. Add beans and remaining ingredients. Lock lid.
4. Press the Bean button and cook for the default time of 30 minutes. When timer beeps, let pressure release naturally for 10 minutes. Quick-release any additional pressure until float valve drops and then unlock lid.
5. Press Sauté button, press Adjust button to change the temperature to Less, and simmer bean mixture unlidded for 10 minutes to thicken.
6. With a slotted spoon, transfer beans to a serving bowl.

Bowtie Pasta With Pesto

Servings:6 | Cooking Time: 4 Minutes

Ingredients:
- 1 pound bowtie pasta
- ¾ cup pesto
- ¼ cup grated Parmesan cheese

Directions:
1. Place macaroni in an even layer in Instant Pot. Pour enough water to come about ¼" over pasta. Lock lid.
2. Press the Manual button and adjust time to 4 minutes. When the timer beeps, let the pressure release naturally for 3 minutes. Quick-release any additional pressure until float valve drops and lid unlocks.
3. Drain any residual water except for 2 tablespoons; transfer pasta and reserved cooking water to a serving bowl. Combine with pesto. Garnish with Parmesan cheese and serve.

Carrot & Chickpea Boil With Tomatoes

Servings: 4 | Cooking Time: 25 Minutes

Ingredients:
- ½ cup button mushrooms, chopped
- 1 cup canned chickpeas
- 1 onion, peeled, chopped
- 1 lb string beans, trimmed
- 1 apple, cubed
- ½ cup raisins
- 2 carrots, chopped
- 2 garlic cloves, crushed
- 4 cherry tomatoes
- 1 tbsp grated ginger
- ½ cup orange juice

Directions:
1. Place mushrooms, chickpeas, onion, beans, apple, raisins, carrots, garlic, cherry tomatoes, ginger, and orange juice in the Instant Pot. Pour enough water to cover. Cook on High Pressure for 8 minutes. Do a natural release for 10 minutes. Serve warm.

Traditional Italian Pesto

Servings: 4 | Cooking Time: 20 Minutes

Ingredients:
- 3 zucchini, peeled, chopped
- 1 eggplant, peeled, chopped
- 3 red bell peppers, chopped
- ½ cup basil-tomato juice
- ½ tbsp salt
- 2 tbsp olive oil

Directions:
1. Add zucchini, eggplant, bell peppers, basil-tomato juice, salt, and olive oil to the pot and give it a good stir. Pour 1 cup of water. Seal the lid and cook on High Pressure for 15 minutes. Do a quick release. Set aside to cool completely. Serve as a cold salad or a side dish.

Curly Kale Soup

Servings: 4 | Cooking Time: 20 Minutes

Ingredients:
- 4 cups curly kale
- 2 tbsp Ginger, minced
- 4 Garlic cloves, minced
- 1 tbsp Mustard seeds
- 1 tbsp Olive oil
- 1 cup Heavy cream
- 2 cups vegetable broth
- 1 tbsp Cumin powder

Directions:
1. Warm olive oil in your Instant Pot on Sauté. Place the mustard seeds, garlic, ginger, cumin powder, vegetable broth, curly kale, and heavy cream. Seal the lid, select Manual, and cook for 10 minutes on High pressure. When done, perform a quick pressure release and unlock the lid. Serve warm.

Sautéed Spinach With Roquefort Cheese

Servings: 2 | Cooking Time: 10 Minutes

Ingredients:
- ½ cup Roquefort cheese, crumbled
- 9 oz fresh spinach
- 2 leeks, chopped
- 2 red onions, chopped
- 2 garlic cloves, crushed
- 3 tbsp olive oil

Directions:
1. Grease the inner pot with oil. Stir-fry leeks, garlic, and onions for about 5 minutes on Sauté. Add spinach and give it a good stir. Press Cancel, transfer to a serving dish, and sprinkle with Roquefort cheese. Serve right away.

Mushroom & Gouda Cheese Pizza

Servings: 4 | Cooking Time: 30 Minutes

Ingredients:
- 4 oz button mushrooms, chopped
- ½ cup grated gouda cheese
- 1 pizza crust
- ½ cup tomato paste
- 1 tbsp sugar
- 1 tbsp dried oregano
- 2 tbsp olive oil
- 12 olives
- 1 cup arugula

Directions:
1. Grease the bottom of a baking dish with one tbsp of olive oil. Line some parchment paper. Flour the working surface and roll out the pizza crust to the approximate size of your Instant Pot. Gently fit the dough in the previously prepared baking dish.
2. In a bowl, combine tomato paste, ¼ cup water, sugar, and oregano. Spread the mixture over the crust, make a layer with button mushrooms and grated gouda. Add a trivet inside the pot and pour in 1 cup water. Seal the lid and cook for 15 minutes on High Pressure. Do a quick release. Sprinkle the pizza with the remaining oil and top with olives and arugula. Serve.

Cheddar Cheese Sauce With Broccoli

Servings: 4 | Cooking Time: 15 Minutes

Ingredients:
- 1 cup broccoli, chopped
- 1 cup cream cheese
- 1 cup cheddar, shredded
- 3 cups chicken broth
- Salt and pepper to taste
- 2 tsp dried rosemary

Directions:
1. Mix broccoli, cream cheese, cheddar, broth, salt, pepper, and rosemary in a large bowl. Pour the mixture into the Instant Pot. Seal the lid and cook on High Pressure for 8 minutes. Do a quick release. Store for up to 5 days.

English Vegetable Potage

Servings: 4 | Cooking Time: 50 Minutes

Ingredients:
- 1 lb potatoes, cut into bite-sized pieces
- 2 carrots, peeled, chopped
- 3 celery stalks, chopped
- 2 onions, peeled, chopped
- 1 zucchini, sliced
- A handful of celery leaves
- 2 tbsp butter, unsalted
- 3 tbsp olive oil
- 2 cups vegetable broth
- 1 tbsp paprika
- Salt and pepper to taste
- 2 bay leaves

Directions:
1. Warm olive oil on Sauté and stir-fry the onions for 3-4 minutes until translucent. Add carrots, celery, zucchini, and ¼ cup of broth. Continue to cook for 10 more minutes, stirring constantly. Stir in potatoes, paprika, salt, pepper, bay leaves, remaining broth, and celery leaves. Seal the lid and cook on Meat/Stew for 30 minutes on High. Do a quick release and stir in butter.

Mozzarella & Eggplant Lasagna

Servings: 2 | Cooking Time: 30 Minutes

Ingredients:
- 1 large eggplant, chopped
- 4 oz mozzarella, chopped
- 3 oz mascarpone cheese
- 2 tomatoes, sliced
- ¼ cup olive oil
- Salt and pepper to taste

Directions:

1. Grease a baking dish with olive oil. Slice the eggplant and make a layer in the dish. Cover with mozzarella and tomato slices. Top with mascarpone cheese. Repeat the process until you run out of ingredients.

2. In a bowl, mix olive oil, salt, and pepper. Pour the mixture over the lasagna, and add ½ cup of water. In your pot, pour 1 cup of water and insert a trivet. Lower the baking dish on the trivet, seal the lid and cook on High Pressure for 4 minutes. Do a natural release for 10 minutes.

Sweet Potato Medallions With Garlic

Servings: 4 | Cooking Time: 25 Minutes

Ingredients:
- 1 tbsp fresh rosemary
- 1 tbsp garlic powder
- 4 sweet potatoes
- 2 tbsp butter
- Salt to taste

Directions:

1. Add 1 cup water and place a steamer rack over the water. Use a fork to prick sweet potatoes all over and set onto the steamer rack. Seal the lid and cook on High Pressure for 12 minutes. Release the pressure quickly. Transfer sweet potatoes to a cutting board. Peel and slice them into ½-inch medallions. Melt butter in the on Sauté. Add in the medallions and cook each side for 2 to 3 minutes until browned. Season with salt and garlic powder. Serve topped with rosemary.

Plant-based Indian Curry

Servings: 4 | Cooking Time: 20 Minutes

Ingredients:
- 1 tsp butter
- 1 onion, chopped
- 2 cloves garlic, minced
- 1 tsp ginger, grated
- 1 tsp ground cumin
- 1 tsp red chili powder
- 1 tsp salt
- ½ tsp ground turmeric
- 1 can chickpeas
- 1 tomato, diced
- 1/3 cup water
- 2 lb collard greens, chopped
- ½ tsp garam masala
- 1 tsp lemon juice

Directions:

1. Melt butter on Sauté. Add in the onion, ginger, cumin, turmeric, red chili powder, garlic, and salt and cook for 30 seconds until crispy. Stir in tomato. Pour in ⅓ cup of water and chickpeas. Seal the lid and cook on High Pressure for 4 minutes. Release the pressure quickly. Press Sauté. Into the chickpea mixture, stir in lemon juice, collard greens, and garam masala until well coated. Cook for 2 to 3 minutes until collard greens wilt on Sauté. Serve over rice or naan.

Parsley Lentil Soup With Vegetables

Servings: 4 | Cooking Time: 20 Minutes

Ingredients:
- 1 tbsp olive oil
- 1 onion, chopped
- 1 cup celery, chopped
- 2 garlic cloves, chopped
- 3 cups vegetable stock
- 1 ½ cups lentils, rinsed
- 4 carrots, halved lengthwise
- ½ tsp salt
- 2 tbsp parsley, chopped

Directions:
1. Warm olive oil on Sauté. Add in onion, garlic, and celery and sauté for 5 minutes until soft. Mix in lentils, carrots, salt, and stock. Seal the lid and cook on High Pressure for 10 minutes. Release the pressure quickly. Serve topped with parsley.

Indian Dhal With Veggies

Servings: 4 | Cooking Time: 35 Minutes

Ingredients:
- 1 cup lentils
- 2 tbsp almond butter
- 1 carrot, peeled, chopped
- 1 potato, peeled, chopped
- 1 bay leaf
- ¼ tbsp parsley, chopped
- ½ tbsp chili powder
- 2 tbsp ground cumin
- 1 tbsp garam masala
- 3 cups vegetable stock

Directions:
1. Melt almond butter on Sauté. Add carrots, potatoes, and bay leaf. Stir and cook for 10 minutes. Add lentils, chili powder, cumin, garam masala, and stock and press Cancel. If the mixture is very thick, add a bit of water. Seal the lid, select Manual, and cook on High Pressure for 15 minutes. Once the timer goes off, do a quick release. Serve sprinkled with parsley.

Simple Cheese Spinach Dip

Servings: 6 | Cooking Time: 20 Minutes

Ingredients:
- 2 cups cream cheese
- 1 cup baby spinach
- 1 cup mozzarella, grated
- Salt and pepper to taste
- ½ cup scallions
- 1 cup vegetable broth

Directions:
1. Place cream cheese, spinach, mozzarella cheese, salt, pepper, scallions, and broth in a mixing bowl. Stir well and transfer to your Instant Pot. Seal the lid and cook on High Pressure for 5 minutes. Release the steam naturally for 10 minutes. Serve with celery sticks or chips.

Chapter 8 Beans, Rice, & Grains

Chapter 8 Beans, Rice, & Grains

Primavera Egg Noodles

Servings: 4 | Cooking Time: 20 Minutes

Ingredients:
- 1 lb asparagus, trimmed
- 2 cups broccoli florets
- 3 tbsp olive oil
- Salt to taste
- 10 oz egg noodles
- 2 garlic cloves, minced
- 2 ½ cups vegetable stock
- ½ cup heavy cream
- 1 cup small tomatoes, halved
- ¼ cup chopped basil
- ½ cup grated Parmesan

Directions:

1. Pour the noodles, vegetable stock, and 2 tbsp olive oil, garlic, and salt in your Instant Pot. Place a trivet over. Combine asparagus, broccoli, remaining olive oil, stock, and salt in a bowl. Place the vegetables on the trivet. Seal the lid. Cook on Manual for 12 minutes. 2. Do a quick release. Remove the vegetables. Stir the heavy cream and tomatoes in the pasta. Press Sauté and simmer the cream for 2 minutes. Mix in asparagus and broccoli. Garnish with basil and Parmesan and serve.

Butternut Squash & Cheese Risotto

Servings: 4 | Cooking Time: 45 Minutes

Ingredients:
- ½ lb butternut squash, cubed
- 3 tbsp olive oil
- 2 cloves garlic, minced
- 1 yellow onion, chopped
- 2 cups arborio rice
- 4 cups chicken stock
- ½ cup pumpkin puree
- 1 tsp thyme, chopped
- ½ tsp nutmeg
- ½ tsp ginger, grated
- ½ tsp cinnamon
- ½ cup heavy cream
- Salt and pepper to taste
- ¼ cup shaved Parmesan

Directions:

1. Preheat the oven to 360°F. Spread the squash cubes on a baking tray and drizzle with olive oil. Roast for 20 minutes until tender. Warm oil in your Instant Pot on Sauté and add garlic and onion; cook for 3 minutes. 2. Stir in rice, stock, pumpkin puree, thyme, nutmeg, ginger, and cinnamon. Seal the lid, select Manual, and cook for 10 minutes on High. When done, perform a quick pressure release. Mix in heavy cream, salt, and pepper. Top with pumpkin cubes and Parmesan shaves and serve.

Pasta Tortiglioni With Beef & Black Beans

Servings: 4 | Cooking Time: 25 Minutes

Ingredients:
- 2 tbsp olive oil
- 1 lb ground beef
- 16 oz tortiglioni pasta
- 15 oz tomato sauce
- 15-oz canned black beans
- 15-oz canned corn, drained
- 10 oz red enchilada sauce
- 4 oz diced green chiles
- 1 cup shredded mozzarella
- Salt and pepper to taste
- 2 tbsp Parmesan, grated
- 2 tbsp chopped parsley

Directions:

1. Heat oil on Sauté. Add ground beef and cook for 7 minutes. Mix in pasta, tomato sauce, enchilada sauce, black beans, 2 cups water, corn, and green chiles and stir. Seal the lid and cook on High Pressure for 10 minutes. Do a quick pressure release. Mix in mozzarella until melted and add pepper and salt. Garnish with parsley and Parmesan cheese and serve.

Parmesan Risotto

Servings:4 | Cooking Time: 20 Minutes

Ingredients:
- 4 tablespoons butter
- 1 small onion, peeled and finely diced
- 2 cloves garlic, minced
- 1½ cups Arborio rice
- 4 cups chicken broth, divided
- 3 tablespoons grated Parmesan cheese
- ½ teaspoon salt
- ¼ teaspoon ground black pepper
- ½ cup chopped fresh parsley

Directions:

1. Press the Sauté button on Instant Pot. Add and melt the butter. Add the onion and stir-fry for 3–5 minutes until onions are translucent. Add garlic and rice and cook for an additional minute. Add 1 cup broth and stir for 2–3 minutes until it is absorbed by the rice.
2. Add remaining 3 cups broth, Parmesan cheese, salt, and pepper. Lock lid.
3. Press the Manual button and adjust time to 10 minutes. When timer beeps, let pressure release naturally for 10 minutes. Quick-release any additional pressure until float valve drops and then unlock lid.
4. Ladle into bowls and garnish each with ⅛ cup fresh parsley.

Boston Baked Beans

Servings:10 | Cooking Time: 45 Minutes

Ingredients:
- 1 tablespoon olive oil
- 5 slices bacon, diced
- 1 large sweet onion, peeled and diced
- 4 cloves garlic, minced
- 2 cups dried navy beans
- 4 cups chicken broth
- 2 teaspoons ground mustard
- 1 teaspoon sea salt
- ¼ teaspoon ground black pepper
- ¼ cup molasses
- ½ cup ketchup
- ¼ cup packed dark brown sugar
- 1 teaspoon smoked paprika
- 1 teaspoon Worcestershire sauce
- 1 teaspoon apple cider vinegar

Directions:

1. Press Sauté button on Instant Pot. Heat olive oil. Add bacon and onions. Stir-fry for 3–5 minutes until onions are translucent. Add garlic. Cook for an additional minute. Add beans. Toss to combine.
2. Add broth, mustard, salt, and pepper. Lock lid.
3. Press the Bean button and cook for the default time of 30 minutes. When timer beeps, let pressure release naturally for 10 minutes. Quick-release any additional pressure until float valve drops and then unlock lid.
4. Stir in the molasses, ketchup, brown sugar, smoked paprika, Worcestershire sauce, and vinegar. Press the Sauté button on the Instant Pot, press the Adjust button to change the heat to Less, and simmer uncovered for 10 minutes to thicken the sauce; then transfer to a serving dish and serve warm.

Pancetta With Black Beans

Servings: 4 | Cooking Time: 40 Minutes

Ingredients:
- 3 pancetta strips, halved
- 1 cup black beans, soaked
- 3 cups chicken stock
- 2 garlic cloves, crushed
- 1 small onion, cut in half
- 1 bay leaf
- Salt and pepper to taste

Directions:
1. Set your Instant Pot to Sauté. Place in pancetta and cook for 5 minutes until crispy; set aside. Stir black beans, chicken stock, garlic, onion, bay leaf, salt, and pepper in the pot. Seal the lid, select Manual, and cook for 25 minutes on High. When done, perform a quick pressure release and unlock the lid. Discard bay leaf and onion. Sprinkle with salt to taste. Serve topped with pancetta.

Broccoli Couscous

Servings: 4 | Cooking Time: 15 Minutes

Ingredients:
- 10 oz broccoli florets
- 2 tbsp butter, melted
- 1 cup couscous
- Salt and pepper to taste
- 2 tbsp parsley, chopped
- 1 ¼ cups of boiling water

Directions:
1. Pour 1 cup of water into the Instant Pot and add a steamer basket. Place the broccoli in the basket and seal the lid. Select Steam and cook for 3 minutes on High. Once pressure cooking is complete, use a quick release.
2. In a bowl cover couscous with salted boiled water. Let it stand for 2-3 minutes until the water has absorbed. Fluff with a fork and stir in broccoli and butter and adjust the seasoning with salt and pepper. Top with parsley and serve.

Amish-inspired Egg Noodles

Servings:6 | Cooking Time: 4 Minutes

Ingredients:
- 1 bag egg noodles
- 2 cups chicken broth
- 4 tablespoons unsalted butter
- ½ teaspoon salt
- ¼ teaspoon ground black pepper
- ¼ cup chopped fresh parsley

Directions:
1. Place noodles in an even layer in the Instant Pot. Pour broth over noodles. Add enough water for liquid to come about ¼" over noodles. Lock lid.
2. Press the Manual or Pressure Cook button and adjust time to 4 minutes. When timer beeps, let pressure release naturally for 3 minutes. Quick-release any additional pressure until float valve drops. Unlock lid.
3. Drain any residual water. Toss noodles with butter, salt, pepper, and parsley. Serve warm.

Bell Pepper & Pinto Bean Stew

Servings: 6 | Cooking Time: 55 Minutes

Ingredients:
- 2 tbsp olive oil
- 1 onion, chopped
- 1 red bell pepper, chopped
- 1 tbsp dried oregano
- 1 tbsp ground cumin
- 1 tsp red pepper flakes
- 3 cups vegetable stock
- 2 cups pinto beans, soaked
- 14 oz can tomatoes, diced
- 1 tbsp white wine vinegar
- ½ cup chives, chopped
- ¼ cup fresh corn kernels

Directions:
1. Set to Sauté your Instant Pot and heat oil. Stir in bell pepper, pepper flakes, oregano, onion, and cumin. Cook for 3 minutes. Mix in pinto beans, stock, and tomatoes. Seal the lid, select Manual, and cook for 30 minutes on High Pressure. Release the pressure naturally for 10 minutes. Add in vinegar. Divide among serving plates and top with corn and fresh chives to serve.

Bresaola & Black Eyed Peas

Servings: 4 | Cooking Time: 60 Minutes

Ingredients:
- ½ lb dried black-eyed peas
- 3 ½ cups chicken stock
- 3 oz bresaola, chopped
- Salt and pepper to taste

Directions:
1. Place the black-eyed peas and chicken stock in your Instant Pot. Seal the lid, select Manual, and cook for 30 minutes on High pressure. Once ready, allow a natural release for 20 minutes and unlock the lid. Sprinkle with salt and pepper to taste. Serve topped with bresaola.

Barley & Smoked Salmon Salad

Servings: 4 | Cooking Time: 30 Minutes

Ingredients:
- 4 smoked salmon fillets, flaked
- 1 cup pearl barley
- Salt and pepper to taste
- 1 cup arugula
- 1 green apple, chopped

Directions:
1. Place the barley, 2 cups of water, salt, and pepper in your Instant Pot. Seal the lid, select Manual, and cook for 20 minutes on High pressure.
2. Once ready, perform a quick pressure release and unlock the lid. Remove barley to a serving bowl. Mix in apple and salmon. Top with arugula.

Confetti Quinoa

Servings:4 | Cooking Time: 20 Minutes

Ingredients:
- 1 cup quinoa
- 1 ¾ cups water
- ¼ cup lemon juice
- ½ teaspoon salt
- 2 tablespoons olive oil
- ¼ cup small-diced green bell pepper
- ¼ cup small-diced red bell pepper
- ¼ cup small-diced yellow bell pepper

Directions:
1. Add quinoa, water, and lemon juice to the Instant Pot. Stir well. Lock lid.

2. Press the Porridge button and cook for the default time of 20 minutes. When timer beeps, quick-release pressure until float valve drops. Unlock lid.
3. Transfer quinoa to a serving dish and fluff with a fork. Toss in salt, oil, and bell peppers. Serve warm.

Spinach & Kidney Beans

Servings: 4 | Cooking Time: 55 Minutes

Ingredients:
- 1 cup kidney beans, soaked
- 2 tomatoes, chopped
- Salt and pepper to taste
- 2 tbsp olive oil
- 1 carrot, diced
- 1 celery stick, chopped
- 1 onion, finely chopped
- 3 cups chicken stock
- 1 cup baby spinach
- 2 tbsp parsley, chopped

Directions:
1. Heat olive oil on Sauté and stir-fry onion, carrot, celery, salt, and black pepper for 3 minutes. Pour in tomatoes, chicken stock, and beans. Seal the lid, select Manual, and cook for 25 minutes on High pressure.
2. Once ready, allow a naturally pressure release for 10 minutes. Stir in baby spinach, press Sauté and cook for 5 minutes until the spinach wilts. Top with parsley.

Red Beans And Chorizo

Servings:8 | Cooking Time: 35 Minutes

Ingredients:
- 1 cup dried red beans
- 1 tablespoon olive oil
- 1 small onion, peeled and diced
- 1 small green bell pepper, seeded and diced
- 2 stalks celery, diced
- ½ pound chorizo, loose or removed from casing
- 3 cups chicken broth
- 1 can diced tomatoes, including juice
- ½ teaspoon garlic powder
- ½ teaspoon ground cumin
- ½ teaspoon garlic powder
- ½ teaspoon sea salt
- 2 teaspoons Creole seasoning
- 1 cup shredded Cheddar cheese

Directions:

1. Rinse and drain beans.
2. Press the Sauté button on Instant Pot and heat olive oil. Add onion, bell pepper, celery, and chorizo. Stir-fry 3–5 minutes until onions are translucent. Add broth and deglaze the Instant Pot by scraping the sides and bottom of the Instant Pot.
3. Add beans and remaining ingredients. Lock lid.
4. Press the Bean button and cook for the default time of 30 minutes. When timer beeps, let pressure release naturally for 10 minutes. Quick-release any additional pressure until float valve drops and then unlock lid.
5. Using a slotted spoon, transfer beans to a serving bowl. Let cool to thicken and serve.
6. Stir in Cheddar cheese and transfer to four bowls. Serve warm.

South American Pot

Servings: 4 | Cooking Time: 30 Minutes

Ingredients:
- 1 cups brown rice
- ½ cup soaked black beans
- 1 tbsp tomato paste
- 1 garlic clove, minced
- 2 tsp onion powder
- 2 tsp chili powder
- Salt to taste
- ¼ tsp cumin
- 1 tsp hot paprika
- 3 cups corn kernels

Directions:
1. Place rice, beans, 4 cups water, tomato paste, garlic, onion powder, chili powder, salt, cumin, paprika, and corn in your Instant Pot and stir. Seal the lid, select Manual, and cook for 20 minutes on High pressure. Once ready, perform a quick pressure release and unlock the lid. Adjust the seasoning. Serve immediately.

Basic Risotto

Servings:4 | Cooking Time: 19 Minutes

Ingredients:
- 4 tablespoons unsalted butter
- 1 small yellow onion, peeled and finely diced
- 2 cloves garlic, peeled and minced
- 1 ½ cups Arborio rice
- 4 cups chicken broth, divided
- 3 tablespoons grated Parmesan cheese
- ½ teaspoon salt

- ¼ teaspoon ground black pepper

Directions:
1. Press the Sauté button on the Instant Pot. Add butter and heat until melted. Add onion and stir-fry 3–5 minutes until onions are translucent. Add garlic and rice and cook an additional 1 minute.
2. Add 1 cup broth and stir 2–3 minutes until it is absorbed by rice.
3. Add remaining 3 cups broth, cheese, salt, and pepper. Press the Cancel button. Lock lid.
4. Press the Manual or Pressure Cook button and adjust time to 10 minutes. When timer beeps, let pressure release naturally for 10 minutes. Quick-release any additional pressure until float valve drops. Unlock lid.
5. Ladle risotto into bowls. Serve warm.

Cilantro & Spring Onion Quinoa

Servings: 4 | Cooking Time: 15 Minutes

Ingredients:
- 1 cup quinoa
- 2 cups vegetable broth
- Juice of 1 lemon
- ½ tsp salt
- 2 spring onions, sliced
- 2 tbsp cilantro, chopped

Directions:
1. Place the quinoa, broth, and salt in your Instant Pot. Seal the lid, select Manual, and cook for 1 minute on High.
2. Once ready, allow a natural release for 10 minutes and unlock the lid. Using a fork, fluff the quinoa. Sprinkle lemon juice, cilantro, and spring onions and serve.

Salsa Rice

Servings:6 | Cooking Time: 15 Minutes

Ingredients:
- 1 cup basmati rice
- 1 cup chicken broth
- 1 jar chunky salsa
- 1 teaspoon salt
- ½ teaspoon ground black pepper

Directions:
1. Place all ingredients in the Instant Pot. Lock lid.
2. Press the Rice button. When timer beeps, let pressure release naturally for 10 minutes. Quick-release

any additional pressure until float valve drops. Unlock lid.

3. Transfer rice to a dish. Serve warm.

Broccoli & Ham Risotto

Servings: 4 | Cooking Time: 25 Minutes

Ingredients:
- 2 cups broccoli florets
- 4 oz ham, cut into strips
- 1 tbsp olive oil
- 2 tbsp butter
- 1 onion, chopped
- 1 ½ cups arborio rice
- 3 ½ cups chicken stock
- 2 tbsp Parmesan cheese, finely grated
- 2 tbsp parsley, chopped
- 1 tsp lemon zest, grated
- Salt and pepper to taste

Directions:
1. Warm olive oil and 1 tbsp of butter in your Instant Pot on Sauté. Add onion and cook for 3 minutes. Stir in rice and cook for 1 minute. Mix in 3 cups of chicken stock. Seal the lid, select Manual, and cook for 5 minutes.

2. When over, perform a quick pressure release. Stir in broccoli and remaining stock and cook for 5-6 minutes on Sauté. Mix in Parmesan cheese, ham, parsley, remaining butter, lemon zest, salt, and pepper. Serve.

Lentil & Chorizo Chili

Servings: 4 | Cooking Time: 40 Minutes

Ingredients:
- ½ lb chorizo sausage, sliced
- 2 tbsp olive oil
- 1 onion, diced
- 1 cup canned diced tomatoes
- 1 cup lentils
- 3 cups vegetable broth

Directions:
1. Warm the olive oil in your Instant Pot on Sauté. Place in onion and chorizo and sauté for 5 minutes. Add in tomatoes and cook for 1 more minute. Stir in lentils and vegetable broth. Seal the lid, select Manual, and cook for 15 minutes on High pressure. When ready, allow a natural release for 10 minutes and unlock the lid. Serve.

Fresh & Sour Bean Dip

Servings: 4 | Cooking Time: 50 Minutes

Ingredients:
- 1 cup white beans, soaked
- 1 garlic clove
- 4 tbsp olive oil
- ½ tsp oregano
- 3 tbsp lime juice
- 2 tsp ground cumin
- ½ tsp chili flakes
- Salt and pepper to taste
- 3 tbsp cilantro, minced

Directions:
1. Cover the beans with salted water in your Instant Pot. Seal the lid, select Manual, and cook for 30 minutes on High pressure. When ready, allow a natural release for 10 minutes and unlock the lid. Strain the beans and let cool.

2. Place olive oil, garlic, oregano, cooked beans, lime juice, cumin, salt, and black pepper in a blender and pulse until well chopped. Transfer to a bowl and scatter with cilantro and chili flakes. Serve right away.

Chickpea & Jalapeño Chicken

Servings: 4 | Cooking Time: 40 Minutes

Ingredients:
- 1 lb boneless, skinless chicken legs
- ½ tsp ground cumin
- ½ tsp cayenne pepper
- 2 tbsp olive oil
- 1 onion, minced
- 2 jalapeño peppers, minced
- 3 garlic cloves, crushed
- 2 tbsp freshly grated ginger
- ¼ cup chicken stock
- 24 oz can crushed tomatoes
- 28 oz can chickpeas
- Salt to taste
- ½ cup coconut milk
- ¼ cup parsley, chopped
- 2 cups cooked basmati rice

Directions:
1. Season the chicken with salt, cayenne pepper, and cumin. Set your Instant Pot to Sauté and warm the oil. Add in jalapeño peppers and onion and cook for 5 minutes, stirring occasionally until soft. Mix in ginger

and garlic, and cook for 3 minutes until tender. Add ¼ cup chicken stock into the cooker to ensure the pan is deglazed. From the pan's bottom, scrape any browned bits of food.

2. Mix the onion mixture with chickpeas, tomatoes, and salt. Stir in the chicken to coat. Seal the lid and cook on High Pressure for 20 minutes.

3. Release the pressure quickly. Remove the chicken and slice into chunks. Into the remaining sauce, mix coconut milk and simmer for 5 minutes on Sauté. Split rice into 4 bowls. Top with chicken, sauce, and parsley and serve.

Chickpea & Lentil Soup

Servings: 6 | Cooking Time: 40 Minutes

Ingredients:
- 2 tbsp olive oil
- 1 onion, chopped
- 3 garlic cloves, minced
- 2 carrots, sliced
- 1 cup canned chickpeas
- 1 sweet pepper, chopped
- ½ banana pepper, chopped
- 1 cup canned diced tomatoes
- 1 celery stalk, diced
- 1 tsp sweet paprika
- 1 tsp cumin
- 1 cup brown lentils, rinsed
- 2 cups spinach, chopped
- Salt and pepper to taste

Directions:
1. Warm the olive oil in your Instant Pot on Sauté. Add in onion, garlic, carrot, banana pepper, sweet pepper, celery, paprika, and cumin and cook for 5 minutes.
2. Stir in lentils, chickpeas, tomatoes, salt, pepper, and 6 cups of water and seal the lid. Select Manual and cook for 10 minutes on High pressure. Once done, allow a natural release for 10 minutes and unlock the lid. Mix in the spinach and adjust the seasoning. Serve warm.

Spinach & Cheese Filled Conchiglie Shells

Servings: 6 | Cooking Time: 45 Minutes

Ingredients:
- ¾ cup grated Pecorino Romano cheese
- 2 cups onions, chopped
- 1 cup carrots, chopped
- 3 garlic cloves, minced
- 3 ½ tbsp olive oil
- 28-oz can tomatoes, diced
- 12 oz conchiglie pasta
- 1 tbsp olive oil for greasing
- 2 cups ricotta, crumbled
- 1 ½ cups feta, crumbled
- 2 cups spinach, chopped
- 2 tbsp chopped fresh chives
- 1 tbsp chopped fresh dill
- Salt and pepper to taste
- 1 cup shredded cheddar

Directions:
1. Warm olive oil on Sauté. Add in onions, carrots, and garlic and cook for 5 minutes until tender. Stir in tomatoes and cook for another 10 minutes. Remove to a bowl. Wipe the pot with a damp cloth, add pasta, and cover with enough water. Seal the lid and cook for 5 minutes on High Pressure. Do a quick release and drain the pasta. Lightly grease olive oil on a baking sheet.

2. In a bowl, combine feta and ricotta cheese. Add in spinach, Pecorino Romano cheese, dill, chives, salt, and pepper and stir. Using a spoon, fill the conchiglie shells with the mixture. Spread 4 cups of the tomato sauce on a baking sheet. Place the stuffed shells over with seam-sides down and sprinkle cheddar cheese on the top. Cover with aluminum foil.

3. Pour 1 cup of water into the cooker and insert a trivet. Lower the baking dish onto the trivet. Seal the lid and cook for 15 minutes on High Pressure. Do a quick release. Take away the foil. Top with the remaining tomato sauce before serving.

Coconut Rice Breakfast

Servings: 4 | Cooking Time: 25 Minutes

Ingredients:
- 1 cup brown rice
- 1 cup water
- 1 cup coconut milk
- ½ cup coconut chips
- ¼ cup walnuts, chopped
- ¼ cup raisins
- ¼ tsp cinnamon powder
- ½ cup maple syrup

Directions:
1. Place the rice and water in your Instant Pot. Seal the lid, select Manual, and cook for 15 minutes on High. When ready, perform a quick pressure release and unlock the lid. Stir in coconut milk, coconut chips, raisins, cinnamon, and maple syrup. Seal the lid, select Manual, and cook for another 5 minutes on High pressure. When over, perform a quick pressure release. Top with walnuts.

Avocado & Cherry Tomato Jasmine Rice

Servings: 6 | Cooking Time: 25 Minutes

Ingredients:
- 2 avocados, chopped
- ½ lb cherry tomatoes, halved
- 2 cups jasmine rice
- 2 tsp olive oil
- ½ tsp salt
- 2 tbsp cilantro, chopped

Directions:
1. Place the rice, 2 cups water, olive oil, and salt in your Instant Pot and stir. Seal the lid, select Manual, and cook for 4 minutes on High pressure. Once done, allow a natural release for 10 minutes and unlock the lid. Using a fork, fluff the rice and add in avocados and cherry tomatoes. Top with cilantro and serve.

Bean Pasta With Vegetables

Servings: 4 | Cooking Time: 30 Minutes

Ingredients:
- 1 cup butternut squash, shredded
- 1 lb penne pasta
- 1 cup pasta sauce
- 1 cup canned white beans
- ½ cup frozen lima beans
- ½ cup black olives, sliced
- 1 cup baby spinach
- ½ zucchini, sliced
- ½ tsp garlic powder
- ½ tsp onion powder
- ½ tsp ground nutmeg
- ½ tsp oregano
- ½ tbsp Italian seasoning

Directions:
1. Place pasta, 3 cups of water, butternut squash, and pasta sauce in your Instant Pot. Seal the lid, select Manual, and cook for 4 minutes on High. When done, allow a natural release for 10 minutes and unlock the lid. Stir in white beans, lima beans, olives, spinach, zucchini, garlic powder, onion powder, nutmeg, oregano, and Italian seasoning and press Sauté. Cook for 5-6 minutes and adjust the seasoning. Serve right away.

Four-cheese Traditional Italian Pasta

Servings: 6 | Cooking Time: 20 Minutes

Ingredients:
- ¼ cup goat cheese, chopped
- ¼ cup grated Pecorino
- ½ cup grated Parmesan
- 1 cup heavy cream
- ½ cup grated gouda cheese
- ¼ cup butter, softened
- 1 tbsp Italian seasoning mix
- 1 cup vegetable broth
- 1 lb tagliatelle pasta

Directions:
1. Place the tagliatelle in your Instant Pot and cover with water. Seal the lid and cook on Manual for 4 minutes. Drain and set aside. In the pot, mix goat cheese, heavy cream, gouda cheese, broth, butter, and Italian seasoning. Press Sauté and cook for 4 minutes. Stir in the tagliatelle and Pecorino cheese and let simmer for 2 minutes. Top with Parmesan cheese and serve.

Mexican Pinto Beans

Servings: 4 | Cooking Time: 45 Minutes

Ingredients:
- 1 chipotle pepper in adobo sauce, minced
- 1 cup dried pinto beans
- 1 tbsp onion powder
- 2 tbsp garlic powder
- 1 tbsp chili powder
- 1 tsp ground cumin
- 1 tsp Mexican oregano
- Salt and pepper to taste
- 2 tbsp cilantro, chopped

Directions:

1. Place pinto beans, onion powder, garlic powder, cumin, chili powder, chipotle pepper, Mexican oregano, salt, and pepper in your Instant Pot. Pour in 3 cups of water. Seal the lid, select Manual, and cook for 25 minutes on High pressure. When ready, allow a natural release for 10 minutes and unlock the lid. Serve topped with cilantro.

Quinoa Bowls With Broccoli & Pesto

Servings: 2 | Cooking Time: 15 Minutes

Ingredients:
- 1 bunch baby heirloom carrots, peeled
- 1 cup quinoa
- 2 cups vegetable broth
- Salt and pepper to taste
- 1 potato, peeled, cubed
- 10 oz broccoli florets
- ¼ cabbage, chopped
- 2 eggs
- 1 avocado, sliced
- ¼ cup pesto sauce
- Lemon wedges, for serving

Directions:

1. In your Instant Pot, mix the vegetable broth, pepper, quinoa, and salt. Set a trivet on top of the quinoa and place a steamer basket on the trivet. Mix carrots, potato, eggs, and broccoli in the steamer basket. Seal the lid and cook for 1 minute on High Pressure. Quick-release the pressure. Remove the trivet and basket from the pot.

2. Set the eggs in a bowl of ice water. Then peel and halve them. Fluff the quinoa. In two bowls, equally divide avocado, quinoa, broccoli, eggs, carrots, potato, cabbage, and pesto dollop. Serve with lemon wedges.

Chapter 9 Desserts & Drinks

Homemade Walnut Layer Cake

Servings: 6 | Cooking Time: 25 Minutes

Ingredients:
- ½ cup vanilla pudding powder
- 3 standard cake crusts
- ¼ cup granulated sugar
- 4 cups milk
- 10.5 oz chocolate chips
- ¼ cup walnuts, minced

Directions:
1. Combine vanilla powder, sugar, and milk in the inner pot. Cook until the pudding thickens, stirring constantly on Sauté. Remove from the steel pot. Place one crust into a springform pan. Pour half of the pudding and sprinkle with minced walnuts and chocolate chips. Cover with another crust and repeat the process. Finish with the final crust and wrap in foil.
2. Insert the trivet, pour in 1 cup of water, and place springform pan on top. Seal the lid and cook for 10 minutes on High Pressure. Do a quick release. Refrigerate.

Banana Chocolate Bars

Servings: 6 | Cooking Time: 25 Minutes

Ingredients:
- ½ cup almond butter
- 3 bananas
- 2 tbsp cocoa powder

Directions:
1. Place the bananas and almond butter in a bowl and mash finely with a fork. Add the cocoa powder and stir until well combined. Grease a baking dish. Pour the banana and almond butter into the dish. Pour 1 cup water into the cooker and lower a trivet. Place the baking dish on the trivet and seal the lid. Select Pressure Cook for 15 minutes on High. When it goes off, do a quick release. Let cool for a few minutes before cutting into squares.

Spiced Red Wine–poached Pears

Servings:4 | Cooking Time: 13 Minutes

Ingredients:
- 4 ripe but still firm pears
- 2 tablespoons fresh lemon juice
- 4 cups dry red wine
- ½ cup freshly squeezed orange juice
- 2 teaspoons grated orange zest
- ¼ cup sugar
- 1 cinnamon stick
- ½ teaspoon ground cloves
- ½ teaspoon ground ginger
- 1 sprig fresh mint

Directions:
1. Rinse and peel the pears leaving the stem. Using a corer or melon baller, remove the cores from underneath without going through the top so you can maintain the stem. Brush the pears inside and out with the lemon juice.
2. Combine the wine, orange juice, orange zest, sugar, cinnamon stick, cloves, and ginger in Instant Pot. Press the Sauté button and then hit the Adjust button to change the temperature to More. Bring to a slow boil in about 3–5 minutes; stir to blend and dissolve the sugar. Carefully place the pears in liquid. Press Adjust button to change temperature to Less and simmer unlidded for 5 additional minutes. Lock lid.
3. Press Manual button and adjust time to 3 minutes. Use the Pressure button to set the pressure to Low. When the timer beeps, quick-release pressure until float valve drops and then unlock lid.
4. Use a slotted spoon to transfer the pears to a serving platter. Garnish with mint sprig.

Festive Fruitcake

Servings:8 | Cooking Time: 20 Minutes

Ingredients:
- 1 can crushed pineapple, including juice
- ½ cup raisins
- ½ cup dried unsweetened cherries
- ½ cup pitted and diced dates
- 1 cup pecan halves
- ½ cup chopped walnuts
- ½ cup unsweetened coconut flakes
- ½ cup sugar
- ¼ cup melted butter, cooled
- 2 teaspoons vanilla extract
- 2 tablespoons fresh orange juice
- 4 large eggs
- 1 cup all-purpose flour
- 2 teaspoons baking powder
- ¼ teaspoon salt
- ¼ teaspoon ground nutmeg
- 1 cup water

Directions:

1. In a medium bowl, combine all ingredients except water until well mixed. Grease a 6" cake pan. Press mixture into the pan.

2. Pour 1 cup water into the Instant Pot. Insert trivet. Lower 6" pan onto trivet. Lock lid.

3. Press the Manual button and adjust time to 20 minutes. When timer beeps, let pressure release naturally for 10 minutes. Quick-release any additional pressure until float valve drops and then unlock lid.

4. Remove fruitcake from Instant Pot and transfer to a cooling rack. Refrigerate covered overnight. Flip onto a cutting board, slice, and serve.

Orange New York Cheesecake

Servings: 6 | Cooking Time: 1 Hour + Freezing Time

Ingredients:
- For the crust
- 1 cup graham crackers crumbs
- 2 tbsp butter, melted
- 1 tsp sugar
- For the filling
- 2 cups cream cheese
- ½ cup sugar
- 1 tsp vanilla extract
- Zest from 1 orange
- A pinch of salt
- 2 eggs

Directions:

1. Fold a 20-inch piece of aluminum foil in half lengthwise twice and set on the Instant Pot. Grease a parchment paper and line it to a cake pan. In a bowl, combine melted butter, sugar, and graham crackers. Press into the bottom and about ⅓ up the sides of the pan. Transfer the pan to the freezer as you prepare the filling.

2. In a separate bowl, beat sugar, cream cheese, salt, orange zest, and vanilla until smooth. Beat eggs into the filling, one at a time. Stir until combined. Add the filling over the chilled crust in the pan. Add 1 cup water and set a trivet into the pot. Put the pan on the trivet.

3. Seal the lid, press Cake, and cook for 40 minutes on High. Release the pressure quickly. Cool the cheesecake and then transfer it to the refrigerator for 3 hours. Use a paring knife to run along the edges between the pan and cheesecake to remove the cheesecake and set to the plate.

Cinnamon Applesauce

Servings:8 | Cooking Time: 8 Minutes

Ingredients:
- 3 pounds apples (any variety), cored and chopped
- 1 teaspoon ground cinnamon
- ½ teaspoon ground allspice
- ½ cup granulated sugar
- ⅛ teaspoon salt
- ½ cup freshly squeezed orange juice
- ⅓ cup water

Directions:

1. Place all ingredients in the Instant Pot.

2. Press the Manual or Pressure Cook button and adjust time to 8 minutes. When timer beeps, quick-release pressure until float valve drops. Unlock lid.

3. Use an immersion blender to blend ingredients in pot until desired consistency is reached. Serve warm or cold.

Quick Coconut Treat With Pears

Servings: 2 | Cooking Time: 15 Minutes

Ingredients:
- ¼ cup flour
- 1 cup coconut milk
- 2 pears, peeled and diced
- ¼ cup shredded coconut

Directions:
1. Combine flour, milk, pears, and shredded coconut in your Pressure cooker. Seal the lid, select Pressure Cook and set the timer to 5 minutes at High pressure. When ready, do a quick pressure release. Divide the mixture between two bowls. Serve.

White Chocolate Pots De Crème

Servings:4 | Cooking Time: 20 Minutes

Ingredients:
- 4 large egg yolks
- 2 tablespoons sugar
- Pinch of salt
- ¼ teaspoon vanilla extract
- 1½ cups half-and-half
- ¾ cup white chocolate chips
- 2 cups water

Directions:
1. In a small bowl, whisk together egg yolks, sugar, salt, and vanilla. Set aside.
2. In saucepan over medium-low heat, heat half-and-half to a low simmer. Whisk a spoonful into the egg mixture to temper the eggs, and then slowly whisk that egg mixture into the saucepan with remaining half-and-half. Add white chocolate chips and continually stir on simmer until chocolate is melted, about 10 minutes. Remove from heat and evenly distribute white chocolate mixture among four custard ramekins.
3. Pour water into Instant Pot. Insert trivet. Place silicone steamer basket onto trivet. Place ramekins onto steamer basket. Lock lid.
4. Press the Manual button and adjust time to 6 minutes. When timer beeps, let pressure release naturally for 10 minutes. Quick-release any additional pressure until float valve drops and then unlock lid.
5. Transfer custards to a plate and refrigerate covered for 2 hours. Serve.

Cottage Cheesecake With Strawberries

Servings: 6 | Cooking Time: 35 Minutes +cooling Time

Ingredients:
- 10 oz cream cheese
- ¼ cup sugar
- ½ cup cottage cheese
- 1 lemon, zested and juiced
- 2 eggs, cracked into a bowl
- 1 tsp lemon extract
- 3 tbsp sour cream
- 1 cup water
- 10 strawberries, halved to decorate

Directions:
1. Blend with an electric mixer, the cream cheese, quarter cup of sugar, cottage cheese, lemon zest, lemon juice, and lemon extract until a smooth consistency is formed. Adjust the sweet taste to liking with more sugar. Add the eggs. Fold in at low speed until incorporated. Spoon the mixture into a greased baking pan. Level the top with a spatula and cover with foil. Fit a trivet in the pot and pour in water. Place the cake pan on the trivet.
2. Seal the lid. Select Manual and cook for 15 minutes. Mix the sour cream and 1 tbsp of sugar. Set aside. Once the timer has gone off, do a natural pressure release for 10 minutes. Use a spatula to spread the sour cream mixture on the warm cake. Let cool. Top with strawberries.

Chocolate Cherry Soda Pop Cupcakes

Servings:12 | Cooking Time: 18 Minutes

Ingredients:
- Cupcakes
- ½ box moist chocolate cake mix
- 6 ounces (½ can) cherry soda
- 2 cups water
- Chocolate Icing
- 4 ounces cream cheese, softened
- ¼ cup unsweetened cocoa powder
- 4 tablespoons unsalted butter, softened
- ½ teaspoon vanilla extract
- ⅛ teaspoon salt
- 2 cups confectioners' sugar

Directions:
1. Grease twelve silicone cupcake liners.
2. In a medium bowl, combine cake mix and cherry soda. Spoon mixture into prepared cupcake liners.
3. Add water to the Instant Pot and insert steam rack. Place six cupcake liners on steam rack. Lock lid.
4. Press the Manual or Pressure Cook button and adjust time to 9 minutes. When timer beeps, quick-release pressure until float valve drops. Unlock lid. Transfer cupcakes to a cooling rack. Repeat cooking process with remaining six cupcake liners.
5. In a medium mixing bowl, cream together cream cheese, cocoa powder, butter, vanilla, and salt. Blend in sugar until smooth. If icing is too loose, add a little more sugar. If icing is too thick, add a little milk.
6. Let cupcakes cool for at least 30 minutes until they reach room temperature, then spread icing on cooled cupcakes. Serve.

Hot Cocoa Brownies

Servings:6 | Cooking Time: 25 Minutes

Ingredients:
- 2 large eggs, beaten
- ¼ cup all-purpose flour
- 2 packets instant hot cocoa mix
- ⅓ cup granulated sugar
- 2 teaspoons baking powder
- 1 teaspoon baking soda
- ⅛ teaspoon salt
- 4 tablespoons unsalted butter, melted
- ⅓ cup mini marshmallows
- 1 cup water

Directions:
1. Grease a 6" cake pan.
2. In a large bowl, combine eggs, flour, hot cocoa mix, sugar, baking powder, baking soda, and salt. Stir in butter and then fold in mini marshmallows. Do not overmix. Pour batter into prepared cake pan.
3. Add water to the Instant Pot and insert steam rack. Place cake pan on top of steam rack. Lock lid.
4. Press the Manual or Pressure Cook button and adjust time to 25 minutes. When timer beeps, let pressure release naturally for 10 minutes. Quick-release any additional pressure until float valve drops. Unlock lid.
5. Remove cake pan from pot and transfer to a cooling rack to cool 10 minutes.
6. Flip brownies onto a serving platter. Let cool completely 30 minutes. Slice and serve.

Spiced & Warming Mulled Wine

Servings: 6 | Cooking Time: 20 Minutes

Ingredients:
- 3 cups red wine
- 2 tangerines, sliced
- ¼ cup honey
- 6 whole cloves
- 6 whole black peppercorns
- 2 cardamom pods
- 8 cinnamon sticks
- 1 tsp fresh ginger, grated
- 1 tsp ground cinnamon

Directions:
1. Add red wine, honey, cardamom, 2 cinnamon sticks, cloves, tangerine slices, ginger, and peppercorns. Seal the lid and cook for 5 minutes on High Pressure. Release pressure naturally for 10 minutes. Using a fine mesh strainer, strain the wine. Discard spices. Divide the warm wine into glasses. Garnish with cinnamon sticks to serve.

Walnut & Pumpkin Tart

Servings: 6 | Cooking Time: 70 Minutes

Ingredients:
- 1 cup packed shredded pumpkin
- 3 eggs
- ½ cup sugar
- 1 cup flour
- ½ cup half-and-half
- ¼ cup olive oil
- 1 tsp baking powder
- 1 tsp vanilla extract
- 1 tsp ground cinnamon
- ½ tsp ground nutmeg
- ½ cup chopped walnuts
- 2 cups water
- Frosting:
- 4 oz cream cheese, room temperature
- 8 tbsp butter
- ½ cup confectioners sugar
- ½ tsp vanilla extract
- ½ tsp salt

Directions:

1. In a bowl, beat eggs and sugar to get a smooth mixture. Mix in oil, flour, vanilla extract, cinnamon, half-and-half, baking powder, and nutmeg. Stir well to obtain a fluffy batter. Fold walnuts and pumpkin through the batter. Add batter into a cake pan and cover with aluminum foil. Into the pot, add 1 cup water and set a trivet. Lay cake pan onto the trivet.

2. Seal the lid, select Manual, and cook on High Pressure for 40 minutes. Release pressure naturally for 10 minutes. Beat cream cheese, confectioners' sugar, salt, vanilla, and butter in a bowl until smooth. Place in the refrigerator until needed. Remove cake from the pan and transfer to a wire rack to cool. Over the cake, spread frosting and apply a topping of shredded carrots.

Butterscotch Crème Brûlée

Servings:4 | Cooking Time: 20 Minutes

Ingredients:
- 4 large egg yolks
- 2 tablespoons sugar
- Pinch of salt
- ¼ teaspoon vanilla extract
- 1½ cups half-and-half
- ¾ cup butterscotch chips
- 2 cups water
- ½ cup superfine sugar

Directions:

1. In a small bowl, whisk together egg yolks, sugar, salt, and vanilla. Set aside.

2. In saucepan over medium-low heat, heat half-and-half until you reach a low simmer. Whisk a spoonful into the egg mixture to temper the eggs, then slowly add the egg mixture back into the saucepan with remaining half-and-half. Add butterscotch chips and continually stir on simmer until butterscotch is melted, about 10 minutes. Remove from heat and evenly distribute butterscotch mixture among four custard ramekins.

3. Pour water into Instant Pot. Insert trivet. Place silicone steamer basket onto trivet. Place ramekins onto steamer basket. Lock lid.

4. Press the Manual button and adjust time to 6 minutes. When the timer beeps, let pressure release naturally for 10 minutes. Quick-release any additional pressure until float valve drops and then unlock lid.

5. Transfer custards to a plate and refrigerate covered for 2 hours.

6. Right before serving, top custards with equal amounts superfine sugar. Blow-torch the tops to create a caramelized shell. Serve.

Nutty Brownie Cake

Servings:6 | Cooking Time: 20 Minutes

Ingredients:
- 4 tablespoons butter, room temperature
- 2 large eggs
- ⅓ cup all-purpose flour
- ½ teaspoon baking powder
- ⅓ cup unsweetened cocoa powder
- Pinch of sea salt
- ⅓ cup sugar
- ⅓ cup semisweet chocolate chips
- ⅓ cup chopped pecans
- 1 cup water
- 2 tablespoons powdered sugar

Directions:
1. In a large bowl, whisk together butter, eggs, flour, baking powder, cocoa powder, salt, and sugar. Do not overmix. Fold in chocolate chips and pecans. Pour batter into a greased 6" cake pan. Cover pan with a piece of aluminum foil.
2. Pour water into the Instant Pot. Set trivet in pot. Place cake pan on top of the trivet. Lock lid.
3. Press the Manual button and adjust time to 20 minutes. When timer beeps, let pressure release naturally for 5 minutes. Quick-release any additional pressure until float valve drops and then unlock lid.
4. Remove cake pan from the Instant Pot and transfer to a rack to cool. Sprinkle with powdered sugar and serve.

Lemon-apricot Compote

Servings: 6 | Cooking Time: 20 Minutes

Ingredients:
- 2 lb fresh apricots, sliced
- 1 lb sugar
- 2 tbsp lemon zest
- 1 tsp ground nutmeg
- 10 cups water

Directions:
1. Add apricots, sugar, water, nutmeg, and lemon zest. Cook, stirring occasionally until half of the water evaporates, on Sauté. Press Cancel and transfer the apricots and the remaining liquid into glass jars. Let cool. Refrigerate.

Catalan-style Crème Brûlée

Servings: 4 | Cooking Time: 15 Minutes

Ingredients:
- 5 cups heavy cream
- 8 egg yolks
- 1 cup honey
- 4 tbsp sugar
- 1 vanilla extract
- 1 cup water

Directions:
1. In a bowl, combine heavy cream, egg yolks, vanilla, and honey. Beat well with an electric mixer. Pour the mixture into 4 ramekins. Set aside. Pour water into the pot and insert the trivet. Lower the ramekins on top. Seal the lid and cook for 10 minutes on High Pressure. Do a quick pressure release. Remove the ramekins from the pot and add a tablespoon of sugar to each ramekin. Burn evenly with a culinary torch until brown. Chill well and serve.

Banana & Walnut Oatmeal

Servings: 2 | Cooking Time: 20 Minutes

Ingredients:
- 1 banana, chopped
- 1 cup rolled oats
- 1 cup milk
- ¼ teaspoon cinnamon
- 1 tbsp chopped walnuts
- ½ tsp white sugar

Directions:
1. Pour 1 cup of water into your Instant Pot and fit in a steam rack. Place oats, sugar, milk, cinnamon, and ½ of water in a bowl. Divide between small-sized cups. Place on the steam rack. Seal the lid, select Manual, and cook for 5 minutes on High pressure. When done, allow a natural release for 10 minutes and unlock the lid. Top with banana and walnuts and serve.

Chocolate Mint Chip Pots De Crème

Servings:4 | Cooking Time: 18 Minutes

Ingredients:
- 4 large egg yolks
- 2 tablespoons granulated sugar
- ⅛ teaspoon salt
- ¼ teaspoon vanilla extract
- 1 ½ cups heavy whipping cream
- ¾ cups mint chocolate chips
- 2 cups water

Directions:
1. In a small bowl, whisk together egg yolks, sugar, salt, and vanilla. Set aside.
2. In a small saucepan over medium-low heat, heat whipping cream to a low simmer, about 2 minutes. Take out a spoonful and whisk it into egg mixture in bowl to temper eggs. Then slowly whisk egg mixture into saucepan with remaining whipping cream.
3. Add mint chocolate chips and continually stir on simmer until chocolate is melted, about 8–10 minutes. Remove from heat and evenly distribute mixture among four custard ramekins.
4. Add water to the Instant Pot and insert steam rack. Place steamer basket on steam rack. Place ramekins into basket. Lock lid.
5. Press the Manual or Pressure Cook button and adjust time to 6 minutes. When timer beeps, let pressure release naturally for 10 minutes. Quick-release any additional pressure until float valve drops. Unlock lid.
6. Transfer ramekins to a plate and refrigerate covered at least 2 hours or up to overnight. Serve chilled.

Pumpkin Cheesecake

Servings:6 | Cooking Time: 30 Minutes

Ingredients:
- Crust
- 20 gingersnaps
- 3 tablespoons melted butter
- Cheesecake Filling
- 1 cup pumpkin purée
- 8 ounces cream cheese, cubed and room temperature
- 2 tablespoons sour cream, room temperature
- ½ cup sugar
- Pinch of salt
- 2 large eggs, room temperature
- ¼ teaspoon ground cinnamon
- ⅛ teaspoon ground nutmeg
- ½ teaspoon vanilla extract
- 2 cups water

Directions:
1. Grease a 7" springform pan and set aside.
2. For Crust: Add gingersnaps to a food processor and pulse to combine. Add in melted butter and pulse to blend. Transfer crumb mixture to springform pan and press down along the bottom and about ⅓ of the way up the sides of the pan. Place a square of aluminum foil along the outside bottom of the pan and crimp up around the edges.
3. For Cheesecake Filling: With a hand blender or food processor, cream together pumpkin, cream cheese, sour cream, sugar, and salt. Pulse until smooth. Slowly add eggs, cinnamon, nutmeg, and vanilla. Pulse for another 10 seconds. Scrape the bowl and pulse until batter is smooth.
4. Transfer the batter into springform pan.
5. Pour water into the Instant Pot. Insert the trivet. Set the springform pan on the trivet. Lock lid.
6. Press the Manual button and adjust time to 30 minutes. When timer beeps, quick-release pressure until float valve drops and then unlock lid. Lift pan out of Instant Pot. Let cool at room temperature for 10 minutes.
7. The cheesecake will be a little jiggly in the center. Refrigerate for a minimum of 2 hours to allow it to set. Release side pan and serve.

Vanilla Cheesecake With Cranberry Filling

Servings: 8 | Cooking Time: 1 Hour + Chilling Time

Ingredients:
- 1 cup coarsely crumbled cookies
- 2 tbsp butter, melted
- 1 cup mascarpone cheese
- ½ cup sugar
- 2 tbsp sour cream
- ½ tsp vanilla extract
- 2 eggs
- 1/3 cup dried cranberries

Directions:
1. Fold a 20-inch piece of aluminum foil in half lengthwise twice and set on the Instant Pot. In a bowl, combine butter and crumbled cookies. Press firmly to the bottom and about 1/3 of the way up the sides of a cake pan. Freeze the crust. In a separate bowl, beat

mascarpone cheese and sugar to obtain a smooth consistency. Stir in vanilla and sour cream. Beat one egg and add into the cheese mixture to combine well. Do the same with the second egg.

2. Stir cranberries into the filling. Transfer the filling into the crust. Into the pot, add 1 cup water and set the steam rack. Center the springform pan onto the prepared foil sling. Use the sling to lower the pan onto the rack.

3. Fold foil strips out of the way of the lid. Seal the lid, press Manual, and cook on High Pressure for 40 minutes. Release the pressure quickly. Transfer the cheesecake to a refrigerator for 3 hours. Use a paring knife to run along the edges between the pan and cheesecake to remove the cheesecake and set to the plate.

Strawberry Upside-down Cake

Servings:4 | Cooking Time: 35 Minutes

Ingredients:
• 2 cups diced strawberries
• 1 cup plus 1 tablespoon all-purpose flour, divided
• ⅓ cup plus 1 tablespoon granulated sugar, divided
• 1 large egg
• 2 tablespoons unsalted butter, melted
• 1 teaspoon vanilla extract
• 1 cup ricotta cheese
• 2 teaspoons baking powder
• 1 teaspoon baking soda
• ⅛ teaspoon salt
• 1 ½ cups water

Directions:
1. Grease a 6" cake pan. Place a circle of parchment paper in the bottom.
2. In a medium bowl, toss strawberries in 1 tablespoon flour and 1 tablespoon sugar. Add strawberries to pan in an even layer.
3. In a medium bowl, beat egg. Whisk in butter, ⅓ cup sugar, and vanilla until smooth. Add remaining ingredients, including remaining flour, except water. Pour batter into pan over strawberry layer.
4. Add water to the Instant Pot and insert steam rack. Lower cake pan onto steam rack. Lock lid.
5. Press the Manual or Pressure Cook button and adjust time to 35 minutes. When timer beeps, quick-release pressure until float valve drops. Unlock lid.
6. Remove cake pan from pot and transfer to a cooling rack to cool for 30 minutes. Flip cake onto a serving

platter. Remove parchment paper. Slice and serve.

Cinnamon Brown Rice Pudding

Servings:4 | Cooking Time: 25 Minutes

Ingredients:
• 1 cup short-grain brown rice
• 1⅓ cups water
• 1 tablespoon vanilla extract
• 1 cinnamon stick
• 1 tablespoon butter
• 1 cup raisins
• 3 tablespoons honey
• ½ cup heavy cream

Directions:
1. Add rice, water, vanilla, cinnamon stick, and butter to Instant Pot. Lock lid.
2. Press the Manual button and adjust time to 20 minutes. When timer beeps, let pressure release naturally for 10 minutes. Quick-release any additional pressure until float valve drops and then unlock lid.
3. Remove the cinnamon stick and discard. Stir in the raisins, honey, and cream.
4. Press Sauté button on Instant Pot, press Adjust button to change the temperature to Less, and simmer unlidded for 5 minutes. Serve warm.

Simple Apple Cinnamon Dessert

Servings: 6 | Cooking Time: 30 Minutes

Ingredients:
• Topping:
• ½ cup rolled oats
• ½ cup oat flour
• ½ cup granulated sugar
• ¼ cup olive oil
• Filling:
• 5 apples, cored, and halved
• 2 tbsp arrowroot powder
• ½ cup water
• 1 tsp ground cinnamon
• ¼ tsp ground nutmeg
• ½ tsp vanilla paste

Directions:
1. In a bowl, combine sugar, oat flour, rolled oats, and olive oil to form coarse crumbs. Spoon the apples into the Instant Pot. Mix water with arrowroot powder in a bowl. Stir in nutmeg, cinnamon, and vanilla. Toss

in the apples to coat. Apply oat topping to the apples. Seal the lid and cook on High Pressure for 10 minutes. Release the pressure naturally for 10 minutes.

Chocolate Custard

Servings:4 | Cooking Time: 20 Minutes

Ingredients:
- 4 large egg yolks
- 2 tablespoons sugar
- Pinch of salt
- ¼ teaspoon vanilla extract
- 1½ cups half-and-half
- ¾ cup semisweet chocolate chips
- 2 cups water

Directions:
1. In a small bowl, whisk together egg yolks, sugar, salt, and vanilla. Set aside.
2. In saucepan over medium-low heat, heat half-and-half to a low simmer. Whisk a spoonful into the egg mixture to temper the eggs, then slowly add the egg mixture back into the saucepan with remaining half-and-half. Add chocolate chips and continually stir on simmer until chocolate is melted, about 10 minutes. Remove from heat and evenly distribute chocolate mixture among four custard ramekins.
3. Pour water into Instant Pot. Insert trivet. Place silicone steamer basket onto trivet. Place ramekins onto steamer basket. Lock lid.
4. Press the Manual button and adjust time to 6 minutes. When timer beeps, let pressure release naturally for 10 minutes. Quick-release any additional pressure until float valve drops and then unlock lid.
5. Transfer custards to a plate and refrigerate covered for 2 hours. Serve.

Carrot Coconut Cake

Servings:4 | Cooking Time: 20 Minutes

Ingredients:
- ¼ cup coconut oil, melted
- ½ cup sugar
- 1 large egg
- ½ teaspoon ground cinnamon
- Pinch of ground nutmeg
- ½ teaspoon vanilla extract
- ¼ cup peeled, grated carrot
- ¼ cup unsweetened coconut flakes
- ½ cup all-purpose flour
- ½ teaspoon baking powder
- ¼ cup chopped pecans
- 1 cup water

Directions:
1. In a medium bowl, whisk together oil, sugar, egg, cinnamon, nutmeg, vanilla, carrot, coconut flakes, flour, and baking powder. Do not overmix. Fold in pecans. Pour batter into a greased 6" cake pan.
2. Pour water into the Instant Pot. Set trivet in pot. Place cake pan on top of the trivet. Lock lid.
3. Press the Manual button and adjust time to 20 minutes. When timer beeps, let pressure release naturally for 5 minutes. Quick-release any additional pressure until float valve drops and then unlock lid.
4. Remove cake pan from the pot and transfer to a rack until cool. Flip cake onto a serving platter.

Chocolate Chip Cheesecake

Servings:6 | Cooking Time: 30 Minutes

Ingredients:
- Crust
- 22 chocolate wafer cookies
- 4 tablespoons unsalted butter, melted
- Cheesecake Filling
- 14 ounces cream cheese, cubed and softened
- ½ cup granulated sugar
- ⅛ teaspoon salt
- 2 large eggs, room temperature
- ½ cup mini semisweet chocolate chips
- 1 cup water

Directions:
1. Grease a 7" springform pan and set aside.
2. Add chocolate wafers to a food processor and pulse to combine. Add in butter. Pulse to blend. Transfer crumb mixture to prepared springform pan and press down along the bottom and about ⅓ of the way up sides of pan. Place a square of aluminum foil along the outside bottom of pan and crimp up around edges.
3. With a hand blender or food processor, cream together cream cheese, sugar, and salt. Pulse until smooth. Slowly add eggs. Pulse another 10 seconds. Scrape bowl and pulse until batter is smooth. Fold in chocolate chips.
4. Pour mixture over crust in springform pan.
5. Add water to the Instant Pot and insert steam rack. Set springform pan on steam rack. Lock lid.
6. Press the Manual or Pressure Cook button and adjust time to 30 minutes. When timer beeps, quick-re-

release pressure until float valve drops. Unlock lid.

7. Lift pan out of pot. Let cool at room temperature 10 minutes. The cheesecake will be a little jiggly in the center. Refrigerate a minimum of 2 hours or up to overnight to allow it to set. Release sides of pan and serve.

Peachy Crisp

Servings:4 | Cooking Time: 12 Minutes

Ingredients:
- 3 cups peeled, pitted, and diced peaches
- 4 tablespoons unsalted butter, melted
- ½ cup old-fashioned oats
- ⅛ cup all-purpose flour
- ¼ cup chopped almonds
- ⅓ cup granulated sugar
- ¼ teaspoon ground allspice
- ¼ teaspoon salt
- 1 cup water

Directions:
1. Place peaches in a 7-cup glass baking dish.
2. In a food processor, pulse together butter, oats, flour, almonds, sugar, allspice, and salt until butter is well distributed.
3. Preheat oven to broiler at 500°F.
4. Add water to the Instant Pot and insert steam rack. Lower glass baking dish onto steam rack. Lock lid.
5. Press the Manual or Pressure Cook button and adjust time to 8 minutes. When timer beeps, let pressure release naturally until float valve drops. Unlock lid.
6. Place dish under broiler 3–4 minutes until browned.
7. Serve warm or chilled.

Yogurt Cheesecake With Cranberries

Servings: 6 | Cooking Time: 45 Minutes + Chilling Time

Ingredients:
- 2 lb Greek yogurt
- 2 cups sugar
- 4 eggs
- 2 tsp lemon zest
- 1 tsp lemon extract
- 1 cheesecake crust
- For topping:
- 7 oz dried cranberries
- 2 tbsp cranberry jam
- 2 tsp lemon zest
- 1 tsp vanilla sugar
- 1 tsp cranberry extract
- ¾ cup lukewarm water

Directions:
1. In a bowl, combine yogurt, sugar, eggs, lemon zest, and lemon extract. With a mixer, beat well until well-combined. Place the crust in a greased cake pan and pour in the filling. Flatten the surface with a spatula. Leave in the fridge for 30 minutes. Combine cranberries, jam, lemon zest, vanilla sugar, cranberry extract, and water in the pot. Simmer for 15 minutes on Sauté. Remove and wipe the pot clean. Fill in 1 cup water and insert a trivet. Set the pan on top of the trivet and pour cranberry topping. Seal the lid and cook for 20 minutes on High Pressure. Do a quick release. Run a sharp knife around the edge of the cheesecake. Refrigerate. Serve and enjoy!

Rice Pudding

Servings:4 | Cooking Time: 25 Minutes

Ingredients:
- 1 cup Arborio rice
- 1 ½ cups water
- 1 tablespoon vanilla extract
- 1 cinnamon stick
- 1 tablespoon unsalted butter
- 1 cup golden raisins
- ¼ cup granulated sugar
- ½ cup heavy cream

Directions:
1. Add rice, water, vanilla, cinnamon stick, and butter to the Instant Pot. Lock lid.
2. Press the Manual or Pressure Cook button and adjust time to 20 minutes. When timer beeps, let pressure release naturally for 10 minutes. Quick-release any additional pressure until float valve drops. Press the Cancel button. Unlock lid.
3. Remove cinnamon stick and discard. Stir in raisins, sugar, and heavy cream.
4. Press the Sauté button on the Instant Pot, press Adjust button to change temperature to Less, and simmer unlidded 5 minutes. Serve warm.

Appendix : Recipes Index

C

D

Made in the USA
Coppell, TX
18 June 2023

18161674R00057